A Rainbow Book

Peace at Any Price

How to Overcome ———— ———— the Please Disease

Deborah Day Poor, LCSW

Rainbow Books, Inc.
FLORIDA

Library of Congress Cataloging-in-Publication Data

39092 06232509 9

Poor, Deborah Day, 1944-
    Peace at any price : how to overcome the please disease / by Deborah Day Poor.
        p. cm.
    Includes bibliographical references and index.
    ISBN 1-56825-099-1 (pbk. : alk. paper)
    1. Assertiveness (Psychology) I. Title.
    BF575.A85P66 2005
    155.2'32—dc22

                                2004023475

                    Peace at Any Price: How to Overcome the Please Disease
                        Copyright 2005 by Deborah Day Poor, LCSW
                                ISBN 1-56825-099-1

Publisher

    Rainbow Books, Inc.
    P. O. Box 430
    Highland City, FL 33846
    Telephone: 863.648.4420; Facsimile: 863.647.5951
    Email: RBIbooks@aol.com; Website: www.RainbowBooksInc.com

Order Information

    Booksellers/Retailers: Ingram, B&T, Book Clearing House
    Individuals: 1.800.431.1579; www.AllBookStores.com

                                First edition 2005
                11 10 09 08 07 06 05   5 4 3 2 1
                        Printed in the United States of America.

To my sons, Nathan and Jason

As wonderful little boys, they filled my heart with joy
and, as adults, have become two of my best friends.

Contents

Acknowledgments

The journey of writing a book — something many of us want to do — is not a solitary journey. It has been my dream of 15 years to put into print this wisdom of life-long learning. I want to thank the following people who have helped make my dream come true:

Emily Adams, Marti Bauer, Louise Brown, Angie Cooper, Le Arda Day, Elizabeth Du Bois, Sue Flaig, Barb Folan, Sue Foris, Shirley Hermanson, Danielle Jaeger, Covel Jerauld, Tina Magnone, Elaine McLanaghan, Shirley Mills, my son Jason Poor, Jean Richards, Joni Shafer, Nonda Severson, Mary Jane Sheridan, Dora Smith, Deanie Sorahan, Cheryl Ward and Sarah Whitman.

I especially want to thank Bob Hill for teaching me writing skills by patiently editing everything I sent him, and Lana Bruce, my friend and the editor of this book. Thanks to Julia Riley, my neighbor and walking buddy, who gently — okay, not so gently — nagged me into getting this done; Julia is a nurse, author, and speaker who understands the battle with procrastination. Visit her website at www.ConstantSource.com. A special thanks to Betty Wright and her staff at Rainbow Books; she demystified the process of publishing and marketing. Their support and caring helped me make my dream a reality.

And to Tuxedo, my beloved feline friend — a constant source of comfort and unconditional love.

Introduction

How much is too much?

This book is for anyone who avoids arguments, dodges debates, conforms to norms and will do just about anything to keep the peace. It is written to help peace-at-any-price people create the serenity they desperately desire and deserve.

Several years ago, while working in an addiction treatment center, I led a small group therapy session. I asked the alcoholics and addicts in the group to tell me how they picked their wives and girl friends. All of these I-want-what-I-want-when-I-want-it guys had been institutionalized before and were, therefore, treatment-wise.

One asked, "Do you mean the enablers?"

I nodded my head in agreement.

Another fellow said, "You're a counselor, so you know the answer. Right?"

My response was, "I want to hear *your* answers."

The most talkative member of the group blurted out, "It's easy. They're nice. They'll buy you presents, cook your favorite foods, and if you pick a fight with them, they'll make up."

I noticed the other group members were nodding their heads in agreement, and a couple of them even laughed aloud. Since then, I have shared this information with numerous peace-at-any-price clients. I want them to know that their eager-to-please personalities do not give them the peace they value above all else. In fact, these polite, generous, passive beings attract partners who rob them of the peace they want most. They're magnets for temper-tantrum throwing adults. Their easygoing personalities draw self-centered troublemakers to them. So, instead of creating serene lives, they live chaotic, hectic, hellish lives with partners who take advantage of them.

I usually use feminine pronouns to refer to peacemakers and masculine pronouns for troublemakers, since I believe males are more aggressive by nature, and our society has taught them it's okay to be angry but not to be scared or to cry. Females, on the other hand, are more passive and are taught to "keep the peace." However, many, many men are peace-at-any-price people who have attracted troublemakers to them. Reading this book will help both genders create the peace on Earth that begins inside each one of us.

I trace the cause of my peace-at-any-price personality to a crime committed against my great-grandmother. I show how one act of violence affected five generations. Further, I share some of my experiences and acquired strengths in the hope that it will inspire you to take the steps you need to create the peace on Earth that begins inside of you.

Chapter 1

Portrait of a Peace-at-Any-Price Person

Most mental health professionals believe that a person's personality is well formed before he or she attends kindergarten. During the first five years of life we learn to get what we want most by being compliant, assertive or aggressive. With words and actions our primary caretakers reward and punish us and thereby program our subconscious minds.

Over 90 percent of what we do, day in and day out, we do with our subconscious minds; for example, driving a car. If you're an experienced driver, you don't have to consciously think about what you're doing to drive. You simply slide into the driver's seat, put the key in the ignition, buckle your seat belt, push buttons for lights, radio, whatever you need, put the car in gear, your foot on the accelerator and take off down the street. At the end of 10 miles, if I asked you how many red lights you stopped at, you probably wouldn't know; the conscious part of your mind is thinking about something else, while it relies on the subconscious mind to take you where you're going.

The same holds true for interacting with other people.

If, when you were a toddler, you were rewarded for saying "please," "thank you," "yes, ma'am" and "sir," and your parents reinforced their teachings by modeling politeness, you automatically act polite. Also, when your mind was young, like rich, moist soil that has not been worked too much, you repeatedly observed one or both of your parents being considerate of others, then, as an adult, you too are a considerate person. To be otherwise is to put yourself in conflict with your subconscious mind; and this doesn't feel right. If occasionally you say or do something that's hurtful, you most likely correct your mistake by apologizing and vowing not to act that way again. You are appalled by impolite, inconsiderate people and secretly wish they'd be more like you.

Because peace-at-any-price people attract troublemakers, you undoubtedly have at least one person in your circle of family and friends who trounces on your tranquility. This person is quick tempered, argumentative, self-absorbed and impossible to get along with for any length of time. You and other peacemakers in your circle tolerate him and sometimes unknowingly reward undesirable behavior because you fear he'll act worse if you don't. You are uptight in his presence and breathe a sigh of relief when he leaves. At times, you may find yourself wishing him harm. After all, anyone who acts like he does deserves to be punished. For years, you've been wishing that he'd change and act like a nice, normal human being. The thought of changing the way you interact with him has not occurred to you, since everyone knows that *he* should change. After all, he's the troublemaker!

If Nothing Changes, Then Nothing Changes

You've waited long enough for him or her to change. Stop praying and waiting for a miracle and begin to create one. Stop feeling powerless and start taking action. Remember, all you have to do to change a relationship is change the way you interact.

Far too many of us waste precious years while we're waiting for peace and happiness to come to us. We don't have to wait. We can make it happen. We can stop tolerating and rewarding negative behaviors and start doing what's right for us. We can realize that walking on eggshells, giving in and swallowing our feelings has not made anyone, even us, peaceful.

The definition of insanity is doing the same thing over and over again while expecting different results. How many of us so-called peacemakers have tried over and over again to be extra nice to troublemakers, hoping they'd change? Our best efforts failed, but somehow we found the strength to try yet another way to bring about the changes we wanted. Driven by a desire to manufacture peace, we tenaciously set out to alter another person's personality. Nothing changed. Nothing, that is, until we surrendered, gave up all attempts to influence anyone else and concentrated fully on taking care of ourselves. Then, we saw some results. The outcomes were not always exactly what we thought they'd be. Some of them surpassed our best expectations, and all of them made us feel better about ourselves.

If we're painfully honest with ourselves, we acknowledge that FEAR, the worst four-letter word of them all, is the motivating force behind our reluctance to change the way we interact with a troublemaker. We think we'll be worse off, if we don't give in to him. At least, that's what our fear tells us. Some of us have never tried a different approach. Therefore, we don't know this.

Peace-at-any-price people learned our erroneous philosophy when we were children. Most of us lived with an angry, unpredictable parent. We thought our survival depended on not upsetting this parent, who looked like a giant and got what he or she wanted by yelling, hitting, sulking, being critical, sarcastic, impatient and irritable. Naturally, we were afraid of him or her. We were short, not stupid.

Years before we reached the age of reason, the intense experiences we were subjected to taught us to value peace above all else. As long as no one got mad, no one got hurt. That's what our subconscious minds learned. As adults, this literal, habitual, powerful part of our mind that can drive a car, play an instrument or sport, propels us to do what we've always done — keep the peace. Even when our stomach churns, our hands shake, and we break out in a cold sweat in response to what a troublemaker says or does, we think we're keeping the peace, if we keep our mouth shut. Our insides are anything but peaceful. Yet, we keep doing what we've always done.

Here's the problem: This approach to attaining the peace you desire does not work.

Now think about a two-year-old who throws temper tantrums. The tantrums are not a problem unless — what? That's right. He gets what he wants. If someone gives in to him, his subconscious mind learns that stomping his feet, clenching his fist, crying or holding his breath, until his face turns red, gets him what he wants. If this happens, you can be sure that he'll throw another tantrum.

The same holds true for nasty adults. If we, the so-called peacemakers, give in to adults who have their own unique ways of throwing temper tantrums, we reinforce their negative behavior by rewarding them. We're not part of the solution. We're part of the problem. Like two-year-olds, they are not motivated to change as long as they're getting what they want.

If you're like me and the countless peace-at-any price clients I've worked with, the mere thought of standing up to a troublemaker strikes terror in your heart. You've been giving in to him and others like him since you were a kid. Your magical, magnifying mind creates a drama of *what will happen* if you change your reaction to the troublemaker, an imagining dramatic enough to play on Broadway. You imagine the worst. You fear the unknown. We all do. Think about how scared you were the first time you rode a bike, jumped into deep water, took your driver's test, cooked for your in-laws. Repetition of these acts chased the fear away. The same holds true for deviating your dialog with a perturbed person.

A good salesman knows that the most difficult door to walk through is the one that lets him out of his house. If he believes in his product and gets out of his own way, the rest is easy. We all have to get ourselves out of the way. Throughout our life, we are continually challenged to be who we are, to be true to ourselves and to not let the bullies get us down.

By now, you may be reciting reasons why you can't interact differently with the difficult people in your life. Do yourself a favor. Replace the word *can't* with *won't*. By saying *won't* you are, at least, being honest with yourself. If you can talk, you can change the *way* you talk to anyone.

Another thing that keeps peace-at-any-price people stuck in neutral is fear of becoming like the aggressive people in our lives who we silently dislike. When we were children, we vowed that we would never be anything like our angry, aggressive parent. In response to this parent's loud, angry voice, we promised ourselves over and over again, never to be like him or her. Our subconscious minds are programmed by intensity of experiences and repetition. Because we were young and vulnerable, the experience of being with an angry, unpredictable adult was intense. These frightening episodes happened frequently;

therefore, we often reminded ourselves not to be like him or her. Consequently, our subconscious minds, which cannot evaluate information, literally believe everything we think and trap us into being too passive.

Traits of Peace-At-Any-Price People

1. Value peace above all else.

2. Try to avoid arguments, disagreements and fights.

3. Fear anger.

4. Have a history of childhood abuse, abandonment or neglect.

5. Put other people's wants and needs ahead of their own.

6. Silently dislike aggressive people.

7. Do not like to ask for what they want.

8. Attract aggressive partners.

9. Stuff their feelings.

10. Avoid making decisions that affect others (i.e., choose movies, restaurants, etc.)

REFLECTIONS

1. List the names of the adults you were afraid of when you were a child.

2. List the names of people you try to "keep peace" with today.

3. Write about an incident when you rewarded negative behavior in an attempt to "keep the peace."

Chapter 2

Feelings 101

By the time we graduate from high school, we know how to diagram a sentence and dissect a frog. After twelve years of formal education, we've learned — more than once — about the wars that took place at home and abroad. Our heads are full of information that we may never use. But we've never taken a class that teaches us how to manage our emotions.

By then, some of us have lost a loved one or suffered an injury or illness that's serious enough to alter our lives. But nothing we learned in school taught us how to cope with these losses.

While growing up, all of us are subjected to insults and unfair treatment. Very few of us know how to soothe our souls. In fact, we live in a society that teaches us the worst possible ways to manage our emotions. By word and example our parents and teachers have told us to keep our feelings to ourselves. To prove this point, I'm going to give you the first few words of some "don't talk" and "don't feel" peace-at-any-price clichés, and I want you to complete the cliché.

1. If you have nothing nice to say, _____ _____.
2. Don't rock _____ _____.
3. Don't make _____.
4. Silence is _____.
5. Children should be seen _____ _____ _____.
6. Don't air your dirty laundry ___ _____.
7. Keep it _____ _____.
8. Smile and the world smiles with you. Cry and _____ _____ _____.
9. Grin and _____ ____.
10. Go with _____ _____.
11. Let sleeping dogs _____.
12. Keep your skeletons ____ _____ _____.
13. If you're gonna cry, I'll give you _____ ___ _____ _____.

I'll bet that was one of the easiest exercises you've ever completed!

Now review these clichés and think about the ones that are familiar to you and who said them. Can you understand how messages like these from significant people in your life taught you to bury your feelings? Feelings, though, do not magically disappear when we tell them to go away. They do not obey commands or respond to "shoulds." We all feel what we feel — regardless of what we've been taught.

In recent years many therapists have begun to refer to our "feeling nature" as our "inner child." I like the term "inner child" because feelings are as persistent as a two-year-old. There is no wizardry or scientific formula that can instantly control or wipe out an emotion. And, like two-year-olds, the more we ignore our feelings and try to make them go away, the worse they become. In other words, when it comes to feelings, what we resist, persists.

The best way to create harmony with our emotions is to be honest about them. That's why everything from a private therapy session to an honest letter to "Dear Abby" provides some relief.

In the late 1950s, when I was a teenager, my best friend was sentenced to weekly therapy sessions with the school psychologist. Her teachers insisted she go because she was often disruptive in classes. On the day that she kept her appointment with the shrink, I presided over a student counsel meeting. After her session and my meeting, we walked home together. During our two-mile trek, I asked her every question I could imagine:

What did you say? Why were you there? Did he give you a diagnosis?

Perhaps I already had an innate interest in how our minds work. But more than likely, living with an alcoholic father and grieving the early death of my battered mother were the real driving forces behind my curiosity. A safe way to figure myself out was to first figure her out.

She didn't want to talk to me about her visits to the psychologist. One day she said, "You're more interested in this than I am. So why don't I tell him that you'll take my place?"

I agreed.

She made her request, and the psychologist said he'd talk to my teachers. A week later my friend informed me that my teachers told the psychologist that I didn't need his help. Why? My grades were good, and I wasn't a classroom nuisance.

Remembering this incident still upsets me. There were only about 5,000 people in our town and forty-two students in my class. Everybody knew everybody. On warm nights townspeople sat on front porches and identified all passersby and linked them to kith and kin. Some of my teachers knew that my mother had recently passed on; and, both of my brothers had recently used Uncle Sam to make their escape from the home-front battleground. My alcoholic father couldn't even provide for my physical needs. If my back-door approach to the psychologist's office had worked, I might have gotten the help I needed and been spared the consequences of some of the self-defeating decisions I made later.

Ever so gradually, we are making progress in this country when it comes to encouraging people to express their emotions. The American Red Cross has supplied victims of floods, fires and other tragedies with food, clothing and shelter. Today, counselors are also part of their relief packages. Schools and companies solicit the help of mental health professionals when tragedies strike.

We Act Out the Feelings We Don't Talk About

For many years, after I was denied my right to counseling, I alleviated some of the pain I buried by trying to make my surroundings perfect. Instead of dealing with my anger toward my father and the sorrow of losing the person I loved most, I tried to make myself believe that a spotless house and a manicured yard would make everything okay. Giving up this way of thinking was not easy. The vacuuming, dusting, scrubbing, mowing, etc., always made me feel better — at least, for a little while.

Perfectionism is just one of many ways we act out the feelings we don't talk about. Have you ever noticed how many people there are in our society who abuse alcohol, drugs and food? Do you know others who are hooked on gambling, exercise, sex, work, keeping busy or living in cyberspace? To describe these phenomena we have coined a new term: addictive personality.

Babies are not born with faulty personalities. They are born into a society that asked them to do the impossible — don't feel. Consequently, at an early age, we are forced to find a way to medicate the emotions we are not encouraged or even allowed to express.

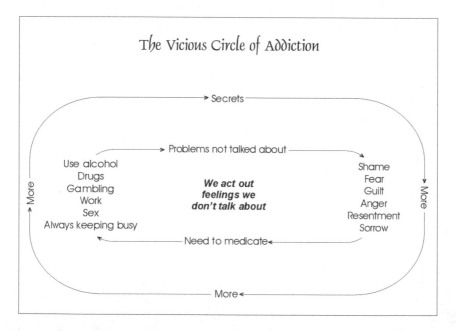

The Vicious Circle of Addiction

This is one of the reasons why 12-step support groups like AA work. In these meetings, addicted people are allowed the luxury of talking about their feelings. They discover that the way out of the vicious circle of addiction is to break the long-standing, self-defeating, don't-talk and don't-feel rules.

Before I had the privilege of becoming a member of Al-Anon, a 12-step support group for loved ones of alcoholics, I didn't know that no one outside ourselves can make us feel anything. Feelings are an inside job. One way to illustrate this truth is to think about a boss who calls two employees (let's name them Art and Steve) to his office. The boss says to them, "Production is down because you're not doing a good job."

The employees leave his office. Art is angry. He thinks the boss expects too much of his workers. Steve is scared. He doesn't want to lose his job. He questions himself and wonders what he can do to improve his performance. Both of them were reprimanded by the same person, at the same time, using the same words and body language, but each man felt something different. Thus we know, when we say, "He or she made me feel 'anything,'" we're lying. No one has the power to make us feel anything, but we all feel.

Feelings, more often than not, are the driving force behind our actions. We feel like we're in love, so we get married. We feel hurt by what someone said, so we change the way we interact with him/her. Because peace-at-any-price people were afraid of an angry adult when we were small, we go to extremes to keep people from getting angry. We avoid angry people, deny our feelings, use a substance or activity to keep our feelings to ourselves and apologize for something gone wrong that was not our fault. When we say, "I'm sorry," what we're really saying is, "Don't get mad. I'm scared. I can't stand it when you get mad." All this walking-on-eggshells behavior is coming from our subconscious minds. These are flight responses that we learned when we were children. Until we become conscious of our automatic, fearful responses, we cannot recognize the adverse ways they are affecting our lives.

What We Run From — We Run To

I often tell my peace-at-any-price clients that there's a type of insurance only peacemakers can get. It's called, "My fault!"

They laugh at themselves when they hear this, since they know the way they think. What they don't know is why they hold themselves responsible for other peoples' actions. If they're interested, I explain that the pay off for this kind of thinking is: If it's all my fault, then I can fix it. Instead of reexperiencing the horrible, frightening feelings of powerlessness that plagued their childhoods, they'd rather assume responsibility for loved one's thoughts and actions, and thereby give themselves a sense of control.

Let's look at Polly, a client I met in a treatment center. Polly had a mean, alcoholic father. When she was young, defenseless and impressionable, she tried to do whatever she could to please Daddy. Today, as an adult, the part of her brain that types sixty words per minute and nags at her when she's forgotten something tries to keep the peace with her husband Tyrone.

Her conscious mind tells her Tyrone is not like her father; he doesn't drink. When she recalls some of her father's worst alcohol-induced violent acts, she gives thanks for her teetotaling husband. She's never acknowledged the similarities between her father's and Tyrone's tempers. She does not consciously know that she's afraid of Tyrone's anger because it reminds her of her father's anger.

To avoid the angry outbursts that she fears most, Polly is willing to do whatever it takes to please Tyrone. This is not an easy task, since Tyrone is a major fault finder. He criticizes her cooking, housekeeping, parenting and social skills. He makes snide remarks about her family and friends. His best weapon, the one that hurts most, is the remark he makes about the weight she's gained. Occasionally, when her emotional pain is unbearable, she defends herself. When she does, Tyrone accuses her of being too sensitive and lacking a sense of humor.

Polly is not always nice. Once in a while she loses her composure, usually over something small and insignificant like dirt on the floor, a spilled glass of milk or something unfinished on her time schedule. She overreacts to these things by yelling loud enough for the neighbors to hear. She doesn't seem to care what anyone thinks, until she's calmed down; then, she feels guilt and shame. These uncomfortable feelings push her back to her peace-at-any-price words and actions.

A big difference between Polly and Tyrone are their frustration tolerance levels. Because Polly grew up in an emotionally unstable family, one that forced her to put other family members' needs ahead of her own, she acquired a high tolerance for frustration. On the other hand, Tyrone, whose parents and older siblings catered to his every whim, is intolerant. Consequently, Polly and Tyrone have this in common: when something goes wrong, they both believe it is Polly's fault!

The Way Out Is Through

I met Polly and Tyrone through their sixteen-year-old daughter Annie. They participated in the family program at New Beginnings, a part of Annie's treatment for anorexia.

Polly and Tyrone wanted to help their daughter. Tyrone wanted us to teach him how to make her eat. In fact, he became impatient and irate with our counselors for probing into their personal lives. As usual, Polly was the self-appointed peacekeeper. She took it upon herself to make everyone calm and happy.

Connie, one of our "eating disorder" counselors, said, "Polly, here we encourage the honest expression of feelings. We know that the quickest way for a family to recover from their problem is to go right through it, kicking, screaming and crying. For this reason, I want you to put your hands under your legs to help you stop patting Tyrone's hand when he wants to express his anger."

Polly looked surprised. She rolled her eyes, as if to say, "You don't know what you're doing. He'll make a fool of himself, if we let him."

Connie, adept at reading peace-at-any-price minds, said, "It's okay. Really. It's okay."

Polly sat on her hands, forcing herself to be quiet while Tyrone spoke.

"Annie's spoiled," Tyrone said, his voice escalating. "We've given her everything. On her sixteenth birthday I parked a brand new, sparkling red convertible in our driveway for her. I don't think she appreciates anything I've done for her."

Connie turned to Annie, an inpatient in the eating disorder program for three weeks. "Have your parents given you everything you wanted? "

Annie stared at the floor and shook her head "no."

"What's missing?" Connie asked.

In a whisper Annie said, "Dad is always so angry. He says mean things to Mom, especially about her weight. She pretends to ignore him, but I know it hurts her feelings. I don't want to be like her. I'm afraid if I get fat someone will treat me like that." Tears slid down Polly's cheeks.

The mother of another client seated next to Polly wiped her face with a tissue.

Polly made herself smile, while Tyrone crossed his chest with his arms.

Over the next few months our staff continued to encourage Polly and Annie to break down society's "don't talk" and "don't feel" rules. We supported them in telling Tyrone how they felt when he resorted to using sarcasm and other forms of put downs he had obviously rehearsed for years. At first, they were scared. They were doing something new. But like anything else, the more they practiced, the better they got at it. They began to accept that Tyrone was Tyrone, and there was nothing either of them or our staff could do to change him. It didn't matter. As long as they took care of themselves by using assertiveness skills, his harsh comments lost their sting.

Sometimes they fell back into their old habits by pretending not to notice his critical comments. Connie reassured them, telling them that this was normal, while encouraging them to tell Tyrone how they felt when they got in touch with their feelings. "It doesn't matter," Connie said, "if it takes days, weeks or even months for you to get in touch with what you feel and bring it to his attention. All that's important is the commitment you both have made to taking care of yourselves."

Polly and Annie made a pact. They recognized that they both often said, "I'm sorry," when what they meant was, "Don't get mad." They promised themselves and each other to take the words, "I'm sorry," out of their vocabularies. They agreed to replace those words with, "I apologize," and to use that phrase only when they sincerely believed that they had done something warranting an apology.

Polly often referred to herself as a Weight Watchers' alumnus. She said she'd lost and regained hundreds of pounds during her adult life. She admitted to using food to stuff feelings and to overeating as a way of rebelling against Tyrone. She was optimistic that her Weight Watchers' participation would bring her the permanent weight loss she desired because now she had new ways to take care of herself.

In addition to using her new, improved communication skills, Annie agreed to attend our outpatient program and to stay on the food plan. Her battle with anorexia was far from over. But we were pleased with her progress and optimistic about her future. The new tools she was using were giving her a sense of having control over more than her weight.

REFLECTIONS

1. What clichés did you hear?

2. Who said them?

3. Do you hear the "don't talk" and "don't feel" messages they convey?

4. What habit(s) do you have that make you uncomfortable?

5. What are the thoughts and feelings you've stuffed that make you want to smoke, drink too much, overeat, use drugs, always keep busy, etc.?

6. Who could you talk to about your thoughts, feelings and habits?

Chapter 3

Ironically, We Are Controlled By Who and What We Try to Control

Prior to coming to our eating disorder treatment center, Polly had no idea how much she'd changed since she'd been with Ty. The changes she noted she had chalked up to the aging process. Her family and friends watched the pretty young girl who breathed life into parties, sometimes attending two or more in a single night, change into a quiet, isolated, overweight, dowdy woman who sought comfort from food. Her transition from the most popular person at the party to a mature matron with a make-believe smile began the first time she went out with Tyrone.

She was surprised that he had asked her out. He was by far the most handsome boy she'd ever met. And he was from the right side of the tracks. She wished she could figure out a way for him to pick her up at someone else's house, and she prayed to God that her father would be too drunk to answer the door. As it turned out, Dad was at the local tavern, his home away from home, so she introduced him to her mother, a perpetually polite person who looked much older than her years.

As they walked from her front door to his car, he took her hand in his. She couldn't believe how good that felt. Before the evening was over, they were French kissing, and he was rubbing his hand across the acrylic sweater that covered her taut tummy and bountiful bosom. She'd never gone this far on a first date. When she returned home, she was surprised that she did not feel guilty. She felt desperate, afraid of what she'd feel, if he didn't ask her out again. She'd given lots of guys goodnight kisses and petted with a couple of them. But she'd never felt anything like this. For the first time, she knew what it meant to be in love.

As the weeks, months and years went by, Polly continued to be enamored by Ty's looks and touch. She enjoyed being the envy of many girls who wanted to date him. And when he touched her, she felt warm, safe, happy and excited, all at the same time.

Cleverly, gradually and continuously, Ty worked to mold Polly into the person he wanted her to be. When she invited him to attend a get together with her family or friends, he suggested they do something else — just the two of them.

She didn't want to disappoint him or miss out on a romantic evening, so she turned down other invitations. Usually, their time alone was not as wonderful as she'd hoped, so she blamed herself. She told herself that Ty probably didn't want to be seen with her because she had gained weight. A few times she was so sure that her weight was the problem that she joined Weight Watchers. But even after she got down to her goal weight and could fit into her old clothes, Ty talked her out of going places with anyone but members of his family and ignored her when they were alone, unless he was in the mood for sex.

On rare occasions, when one of her friends crept into their space, Ty started an argument with them. He baited them into talking about something they felt strongly about, then took an opposing view. Once Louise, Polly's childhood friend, spent a couple of days with them. Ty brought up the subject of abortion.

Louise's response was, "If my mother, who got pregnant with me when she was a teenager, believed in abortion, I wouldn't be here to talk about it." Then, she went on praise her mother's strength and voiced appreciation for the sacrifices her mother had made.

Ty said he was glad everyone didn't think the way Louise did. "If they did," he told her, "we'd live in filth and squalor like people do in India. What's wrong with the world is too many children are raised without fathers, and they turn into fags and women who don't know how to relate to men."

The volume of Louise's voice indicated she was insulted by Tyrone's insensitive, critical comments. Polly had seen Ty like this before. Experience had taught her that there was nothing she could say or do to make things better. She'd learned that the best way to get him to shut up was to stay out of it.

In the past, when he manipulated her into playing "monkey in the middle," she tried to offset his critical comments by changing the subject or tempting everyone with her homemade delicious delicacies. When she did those things, he talked louder and found more ways of insulting her guests. It was as if he were trying to force her to take sides. And she couldn't side with him; it wasn't in her to be so cruel. She'd stopped trying to protect her loved ones, because her attempts just made Ty madder and meaner. She kept her thoughts and feelings to herself. It really wasn't such a difficult thing for her to do; it was the same "don't-talk" and "don't-feel" response she had used when she was a child and her father was home.

After Louise was gone, Polly thought what Ty said was strange, since she heard him take a pro-life stance in the debate with one of their neighbors. During the debate, he seemed to take pride in the fact that he was raised Catholic and said he would not go against the teachings of his church. Polly shrugged her shoulders. She'd given up trying to figure out Ty. There was only one thing she knew for certain: She wasn't going to invite Louise or anyone else to stay with them again. The only way she knew how to protect those she loved from Ty was to keep them away from him.

Polly didn't give up. After many, many episodes, similar to the one with Louise, Polly continued to try to please Ty. Fueled by her desire to have a good marriage, Polly tried everything she could think of to make him happy. She kept a spotless shelter, cooked his favorite foods, served them on time, raised a 'perfect' daughter, kept after their son and said "yes" when she meant "no" in the bedroom. For more than twenty years she tried to be the person he wanted her to be. Nothing worked. Ty didn't change. If anything, he was more difficult to please than he'd ever been. He rarely seemed happy, and he never thanked her for anything she did for him.

Polly didn't complain. She smiled so much that a couple of her friends called her "Smiley." They didn't know that her smile was a form of protection, something she hid behind. As long as she was smiling, no one would ask her what was wrong. She wanted everyone to think she was happy; she wasn't ready to tell the truth, not even to herself. Instead, she minimized, rationalized and justified Ty's wrong doings. In effect, she was telling herself that Ty was not as bad as her father, since he didn't drink and he never hit her.

Ironically, Polly, who tried to control Ty (trying to make someone happy, so that he'll love you, is an attempt to control), ended up being controlled by him. He was still the same person he was when they met. Polly was the one who had changed.

When Annie was admitted to our treatment center, Polly thought this was one of the worst things that had ever happened to her. Now, a few months later, she recognized that her involvement in the family program was a blessing; it had forced her to identify her feelings, to stand up to Ty — take control of herself and her life.

Sometimes Polly balked at the suggestions she heard from members of her group. Occasionally, she said she couldn't interact differently with her husband. Once Connie told her what she had tried to do in the past, that is, control Ty, was the very thing she could not do.

What Polly's group was recommending was difficult, since change is never easy, and the habits Polly had rehearsed for more than twenty years were hard to break, though not impossible. The one person we can all change is ourself.

Our Most Important Relationship Is The One We have With Ourselves

While Polly was trying to please Ty, Annie was trying to find herself. She didn't want to be like her placating mother or resemble her angry, quick-tempered father. Living with them had not helped her to discover who she was or what she wanted from life.

Halfway through sixth grade — when her peers became more important to her than her parents — Annie discovered something that made her the envy of her classmates, helped her to separate herself from her parents and gave her a sense of mastery and control over herself and her life. To do all of this, all she had to do was lose weight and keep it off. Her goal — to look like a super model — was something she could do all by herself and no one could stop her.

Throughout her days, she repeatedly reminded herself of her goal. In her mind she held a picture of an emaciated self. Her goal was also her dream and her escape. This was all that she really wanted from life.

To achieve her goal, she became knowledgeable about how to lose weight. She learned how many calories there are in just about everything — ten calories in a potato chip, fifty in a small apple, three in the glue of a postage stamp, should she make the mistake of licking a postage stamp. Daily, she diligently kept track of everything that passed between her lips, making sure not to exceed 600 calories. When she went over her limit, she felt guilty. She corrected her mistake by increasing her exercise, most of which she did behind her closed bedroom door.

To show off her sleek silhouette, she wore tight-fitting slacks and sweaters to school. To cover her skin and bones, she wore loose fitting jeans and sweatshirts at home. There was no sense in drawing attention to herself from a faultfinding father and a meddlesome mother who would try to make her eat more.

Annie did not know that her subconscious mind was responsible for her "success." No one had ever told her that her subconscious mind worked 24 hours a day and believes what it is told, since it cannot discern messages. She thought she lost the weight because she had more will power and more caloric knowledge than her wholesome-looking schoolmates. She didn't know that the subconscious mind is programmed by repetition and intensity of experience. Since she repeatedly told herself to eat less and exercise more, her subconscious mind made her feel guilty when she ate or relaxed.

Annie was driven and owned by this powerful part of her brain that's strong enough to overcome hunger, if the reward is satisfying. By starving herself, Annie found a way to identify herself, to distance herself from her parents and increase her popularity. Going without food and having occasional hunger pangs was a small price to pay for what she was getting back.

The first thing Annie did when she awoke in the morning was grab her hip bones to make sure they were still protruding. Then she emptied her bladder and stepped on the scale. If she weighed less than she did the morning before, she silently rejoiced in her accomplishment. If she had not lost any weight, according to the scale, she felt disappointed, but not hopeless. This was something she could control and change. Throughout the day, when she needed a lift, something to pick her up, Annie took note of how much looser her clothes fit. From memory, she knew how each piece of her wardrobe fit when she wore it last. The number of garments she had to keep track of decreased as she got too small for them.

One wonders how much longer Annie's anorexia could have gone unnoticed, if she hadn't been in an accident. Because she weighed less than anyone else on the squad, she was awarded the top spot on the high school cheerleading pyramid. One afternoon, during practice, the squad members, who were watching, said she just seemed to collapse, to lose her balance and fall to the left side. Reportedly, her fall was broken when she bounced off one of her teammates, but she still landed hard on her butt on the gym floor. She screamed, and the coach yelled, "Don't move. Don't touch her. Call nine-one-one."

The school principal called Polly. He told her what had happened and said he didn't know how badly Annie had been hurt. Polly's mind was a blur as she drove to the local hospital. What she feared most — something happening to one of her children — was happening now, and her heart was pounding, her hands shaking.

Polly rushed inside the hospital and gave her name to the desk clerk who told her Annie had been admitted. Polly waited. She paced. For the first time in over ten years she craved a cigarette. Finally, a doctor came out and sat down beside her. He told her, "Annie broke her tail bone when she hit the floor. The break is painful though not serious. It will heal. But I'm concerned about what's making her thin enough to sustain such an injury. We want to run a few tests."

Polly agreed, then spent a few minutes with her sedated daughter. She managed to hold back tears of relief while she kissed Annie's cheek, patted her hand and assured her that she'd be all right.

A few days later, when the test results came in and Annie was ready to go home on crutches, the doctor advised Polly to admit Annie to our eating disorder treatment center. Immediately, Polly felt scared of Ty's response. She knew he wouldn't like this, and he'd want Annie to come home where he could take care of her problem. But before she could say or do anything, the doctor walked Polly to the nurse's desk and told the nurse to call New Beginnings and get Annie admitted.

Annie spouted the same complaints we heard from our other anorexic patients — eating made her stomach ache, she couldn't go to the bathroom, she didn't need to be here, she wasn't used to sharing a room, the groups were stupid.

We were empathetic and firm. Knowing that a shrunken stomach cannot comfortably hold a lot of food, we allowed her to eat six small meals a day and to substitute a can of Ensure for one of them. We did not allow her to go to the bathroom alone after a meal. She had denied purging in the past, but we knew that her desperate situation could give birth to new ways for her to control her weight.

Like most anorexics, Annie's progress was very slow. She rarely participated in group discussions, and she silently disagreed with what she heard. To her, staff members and some of her peers were the enemy. We were trying to take from her the one thing that she could depend upon, the only thing that made her feel good.

The girls who had been in treatment longer acknowledged that they didn't go on dates or to parties or out to restaurants, since they wanted to avoid situations where they were expected to eat. They said they focused only on losing weight and getting good grades. Some of them were aware of how much their disease had taken from them, and how they were controlled by it. They admitted that by saying, "Yes," to their disease, they were saying, "No," to life.

Annie was not ready to grasp their viewpoint. Even her injury, which prevented her from being a star on the squad, was not enough to make her want to eat and gain weight. Not yet.

REFLECTIONS

1. Identify someone or something you've tried to control.

2. Did you control him, her or it? Or did you end up being controlled by what you tried to control?

3. Name one thing you can do to improve your relationship with yourself.

Chapter 4

Not Everything That's Faced Can Be Changed, But Nothing Can Be Changed Until It's Faced

It took me a long time to seek help from a mental health professional again. Twenty-two years to be exact. During that time, an "I'm not sure I'm okay" feeling often swept through me. I fought it off by telling myself what my high school teachers said:

"You don't need help. Your grades are good."

After I stopped getting report cards, I found other ways to look good and thereby stifled my uneasy feelings.

In the early 1960s, most women who worked outside their homes were teachers, nurses or secretaries. Many of them wondered what it would be like to be a stewardess. Most of them never found out because they disqualified themselves. After hearing about the airlines' requirements, they decided they were too short, too tall, too shortsighted, too something to join the jet set and lead an exciting, "glamorous" life. But a young woman such as myself who craved positive attention went to the airline interviews and learned that being chosen to fly the friendly skies was a numbers game.

At times, some of the airlines were looking for a few pretty women who met their stringent qualifications. Other times, after they'd purchased many jumbo jets to service hundreds of cities, they hired the tall, the short, the unattractive, the hearing and sight impaired. I worked with stewardesses who were under five feet and over six feet tall.

Besides going to three interviews before being selected to attend a stewardess training school, I also had to talk my instructors into keeping me. They said I lacked the finesse they were looking for. They said I might slap a first class passenger on the back. My fear of being expelled and suffering the subsequent shame made me think quickly. For once in my life I stood up for myself. I said: "I have worked in reservations for two years, and I've never been disrespectful to a passenger. Please contact my former supervisor and ask her about my work performance."

I think they were shocked by my come back and afraid I might file a law suit against them, if they sent me home. Reluctantly, they allowed me to finish training.

In my class, seventeen out of thirty-four graduated. We were all sent to New York City where we got up in the middle of the night to share subways and buses with street people as we found our way, alone, to and from three different airports. For a perfectionist like me, one who feels shame, if I don't do my best, getting to the airports was not as scary as the task of serving 120 passengers drinks, dinner and coffee in less than two hours with no beverage or meal cart and with the help of only one other flight attendant.

Sometimes we landed, standing in the galley, curtain closed, being attacked by the leftover gravy and pudding on meal trays that we had not had time to put away. We quickly cleaned ourselves up, so that we looked presentable in bidding our passengers farewell. Needless to say, we had inside jokes about our "glamorous" job.

Few people knew what our job entailed. Six months after I received my wings, I discovered I was the only one in my class who had not resigned. I think I, too, would have changed jobs. But, at the time, I needed my uniform to help me chase away the "I'm-not-sure-I'm-okay" feeling. Even magazines like *McCalls*, which printed an article stating that stewardesses make the best wives, helped me fight my internal battle with shame. I never read the article, but after four years of flying, I was ready to quit and get married, so I did appreciate the good press that circulated.

Naturally, the qualities that are most important in a mate to a shame-based person such as my self are: good looking, charming and successful. On a flight, the year I decided I was ready to change jobs, I met my Mister All-of-the-above.

Of course, a love based on such superficial qualities is doomed. But at least it protected me from the shame I feared most. And when that wasn't enough, I found other ways to look good. In fact, the possibilities were endless: buy something — a better house, car, wardrobe; join a country club and excel at tennis, golf, socializing; raise money for charity and get my name in the paper. I tried them all, and they all worked for a while. Then, the good feeling wore off, and the shame came back. Because shame is a feeling, something that does not respond to "shoulds" or obey commands, I could not wish it away. Finally, I surrendered. I felt too tired to keep fighting off shame with successes.

I thought about going to a counselor. Then, I talked myself out of it. What would I say? How would I sound? If I talked about my childhood at age 37, I'd sound like a cry baby. And what good would it do? So I prayed. For the first time in over 20 years, I asked God for help. Why not? It was free, and no one would know about it. My prayer was short: "God, if you're there, I need help."

A couple of days later, a friend, someone my husband and I socialized with, stopped by the house and gave me a copy of *Pulling Your Own Strings* by Dr. Wayne Dyer. It didn't look like a book I'd be interested in. But one day I picked it up and began to read; and I couldn't put it down.

I was like the victims Dyer described. I didn't have my say or ask for what I wanted. I didn't even know what I wanted, except I wanted everybody to be nice to one another. I was willing to overlook insults, sarcasm, impatience, sulking and angry outburst directed at me to "keep the peace." I habitually swallowed my emotions to avoid arguments. I didn't know that my peace-at-any-price philosophy was a magnet for troublemakers, people who were not afraid of anger, and my eggshell walk through life was not going to change them or give me the peace I yearned for. Reading *Pulling Your Own Strings* also helped me to acknowledge that I gave my troublemakers mixed messages. Sometimes I rolled my eyes in response to their aggressive words and actions, and other times I felt grateful toward them for protecting me from other bullies — like car salesmen!

You Cannot Solve A Problem With The Same Level Of Thinking That Created It.

I couldn't help talking about my new-found knowledge to anyone who would listen to me. When I told my hairdresser some of what I'd learned from Dr. Dyer, she suggested I read some of her church literature. I thought she didn't grasp what I'd said, since everything I'd learned at church — like turn the other check and put other people's wants and needs ahead of your own — contradicted what the book said.

Three weeks later, when I returned to the hairdresser for a haircut, I handed her literature back to her and said, "I skimmed through it." Of course, that was an out-and-out lie. I had not opened the pamphlets; I was embracing my new knowledge and afraid to read anything that might change my mind. The fact that I wasn't honest with her was evidence of my desire to dodge debate. Naturally, my peace-at-any-price philosophy, which I'd nursed and rehearsed all my life, did not die easily. Fortunately, my hairdresser knew I needed help from other people to change myself; she insisted that I attend church services with her the next Sunday. My eager to please, not-quick-on-my-feet personality said, "Okay . . ."

The sermon was different from what I'd heard at other denominations. For one thing, it focused on living in the here and now. I recalled being turned off by preachers who were hell bent on getting me into heaven when I was having trouble getting through the day. And instead of blaming the devil for our imperfections, this minister explained how our fears interfere with our ability to create more perfect lives. He also stressed the importance of learning to love our neighbor as we loved ourselves — not *more than* or *instead of* but AS. I liked what the minister said. It all made sense. It was similar to what I'd read in Dr. Dyer's book, and I found myself looking forward to Sunday mornings.

Don't Go Into Your Head Alone.
It May Be A Dangerous Place.

Gradually, I gave up my peace-at-any-price philosophy and developed a more mature, assertive way to live my life. It wasn't easy. My subconscious mind doesn't like change, so it made me feel guilty when I stood up for myself. The part of my brain that rides a bike, paddles a canoe and hits a tennis ball much better than it did the first time I tried these things reeked havoc with my conscience when I realized that my wants and needs were as important as anyone else's, especially the ones I loved most. Sometimes it inflicted me with black-and-white, all-or-nothing thinking. It tried to deny my anger and stifle my assertions by making me think that I was turning into my father, a selfish, unreasonable person. Lucky for me, my involvement at church led me to Al-Anon, where I could report what I'd said and done, and find out if I was becoming a bitch. From my support group I learned that a peace-at-any-price person does not immediately turn into a shrew. We are far more apt to fall back into our placating ways.

During this same time period, I found the courage I needed to see a counselor. She asked me to tell her about my childhood. I said my father was a truck driver and an alcoholic who was gone a lot. She allowed me to share how nice my life was when Dad was out of town and gently nudged me into telling her about the Mr. Hyde who destroyed our lives when he was home. She encouraged me to tell some ugly truths by quoting Freud, "Pain does not decompose when we bury it."

When I had left home at the age of eighteen, I desperately wanted to believe that my past was over. I rarely thought about it. I had no way of knowing that I was still suffering emotional pain, since I felt better than I had felt when I was a child, and I couldn't compare my feelings to anyone else's. Even though I disliked talking about my childhood and feeling the pain I buried, I continued to keep counseling appointments; I knew they were helping me to pull my strings.

In time, my counselor suggested that I attend meetings for adult children of alcoholics and other types of dysfunctional families. Because I trusted her and felt grateful for how much she'd helped me, I decided to attend one of the meetings. There, the chairperson handed me a sheet of paper called a "laundry list." It listed the characteristics adult children of dysfunctional families typically have in common.

The characteristic that caught my attention was "a fear of anger." After reading that, I started to realize that I had allowed my husband's angry outbursts to control me. My fear of his anger made me give in to him. During our fifteen-year marriage, I had compromised myself to keep peace with him. Because I did not want my marriage to resemble my parent's marriage, I had taken on the task of keeping the peace. All of my decisions and actions were based on what I thought my husband's response would be. If I disagreed with what he said, I kept my thoughts to myself; I didn't want to make him mad. He never hit me. He spanked our kids, but not hard enough to be accused of physical abuse. There was no logical reason for me to be afraid of him. My extreme fear of anger that controlled my life was coming from my past.

Any time my husband or anyone else raised their voice, uttered angry words, did anything that reminded my subconscious mind of my mean, angry, out-of-control, violent father, I tried to calm them down or somehow escape their wrath. The thought of standing up to them never entered my mind; I was paralyzed by my fear of anger.

For 37 years, I had programmed my subconscious to value peace above everything else. Because that part of my mind cannot reason, it automatically took a peace-at-any-price stance any time someone looked or sounded angry. Consequently, anyone who knew this about me could control me. All they had to do was unleash some of their fury, and I was at their command.

My few-found knowledge inspired me to reprogram my subconscious mind. With the help of a counselor and many support group friends, I gradually overcame my fear of anger. It was the best thing I ever did for myself; it allowed me to find out who I was and what I wanted. In other words, after I stopped being afraid, I stopped surviving and started living. The energy I once used to keep the peace, I now used to better myself and my life. Instead of living my life from the outside in and thinking I was okay as long as everyone else was okay, I began to live from the inside out and to make decisions that were right for me. By giving up all my attempts to make peace with angry people, I found the peace I'd always wanted inside myself.

I was amazed at the amount of time and energy I had at my disposal after I stopped trying to change what I could not change in other people. I used my new strength and freedom to get an education. In graduate school I found the root of my peace-at-any-price philosophy in our family tree. One of my Social Work classes required us to do a genealogy chart. I had little knowledge of my father's family, so I wrote a letter to an elderly paternal aunt and asked her to send me information about the Day family. A few days later, I received a letter from her daughter that reads as follows:

April 11, 1990
Dear Debby,

Mother showed me your letter and asked me to give you the information I've collected on our family. This data comes from a distant relative who visited family members in Holland. He said our great grandmother, Adrianna Lievense, was murdered by her husband, Isaac Timmerman, in Oostburg on October 11, 1876, when Gramma Day was three years old. He was in prison for fifteen years, and before his release Gramma Day came to America alone because she was afraid of him. She worked as a servant for the Day family and later married Jacob, the youngest son who was about twenty years her senior. Supposively, he asked her to marry him after the other family members had left the house; it was because it wouldn't look good for them to live alone together, unmarried. Jacob died when my father was six and your father was four.

I believe the story about her mother's death because Gramma Day spoke fluent English but switched to Dutch when someone brought up anything related to her past. She was a small, religious lady with an eager-to-please personality.

If you need more information, let me know.
Love,
Jane

Immediately after reading Jane's letter, I looked at the 8-by-11 photograph of Gramma Day in my mother's album. In the picture she's about sixty years old, her eyes are sad and her smile is fake. Looking at her picture made me feel some of the pain she buried.

Our lives were similar; we both witnessed domestic violence and lost our mothers too soon, she at age three and me at 13. And we both raised two sons.

She named me Deborah, a Biblical name. I don't remember her because she died when I was two. However, I recall my mother saying that she didn't want Gramma Day to know the way Dad treated her because "it would kill her." And my mother often told a story about Dad driving a brand-new car, one his mother bought, too fast around a curve. He totaled the car when he hit a tree. Gramma Day was so glad he didn't get hurt that she promised him another new car and made good on her promise.

Jane's letter, coupled with what I was learning about human behavior in college, helped me to understand my family legacy and subsequent consequences. At the time of her mother's death, Gramma Day was sentenced to a life of shame. At age three, children think of themselves as all powerful. Consequently, if their family is loving and peaceful, they develop high self-esteem because they think they're responsible for their harmonious family.

In Gramma's case, the reverse was true. Because she obviously never received any outside help to deal with her mother's traumatic death, she undoubtedly found a way to blame herself. In addition to living in fear of a mean man, she buried her pain and held onto shame about a murder that was not her fault. Since she obviously never recovered from her traumatic childhood, she was ill prepared to raise two active sons by herself.

I'm sure that my father and his brother were like all the other children I've known. They did as much as they could get away with. Unfortunately, their mother was not strong enough to set suitable limits and give them consequences for misbehaving. As a result, my father had an underdeveloped conscience that allowed him to drink too much and to beat his wife.

Jane's letter left me with some unanswered questions. Was Gramma Day present when the murder occurred? Was Isaac Timmerman our great grandfather? If not, who was? How did he kill her? With his bare hands or did he use a weapon? I didn't need to know these things to finish my genealogy chart and complete graduate school, so I decided to find the answers later.

REFLECTIONS

1. Do you have a fear of anger?

2. Write down ways your fear of anger makes you compromise your morals, values and desires.

Chapter 5

"Guilt Is the Gift
That Keeps on Giving"
—Erma Bombeck

After I recovered from the shock of running into Polly at "my meeting" — the one I traveled an additional twenty miles in order to avoid running into clients — I smiled at her.

She hurried over to me to and gave me a big hug. I was happy to see her; she'd obviously learned something in our family program that made her aware of her need to attend meetings for Adult Children of Alcoholics and Other Types of Dysfunctional Families.

Polly said she'd been attending meetings here every week since Annie's discharge; and she was surprised to see me. An old, familiar, guilt feeling swept through me, and I was tempted to explain my long absence. But before I said anything, I stopped myself.

My recovery process was teaching me to be internally focused, to stop explaining and defending my actions and to not need approval from anyone to live my life my way. The number of meetings I attended was my choice and my business. The guilt feeling let me know that I had not fully recovered from my past. Some of my people-pleasing personality was still hanging on, or Polly's comment would not have triggered guilt feelings. To make myself feel better, I reminded myself of something I often heard at meetings — "progress, not perfection" — and I recalled some of the progress I'd made.

I remembered how difficult it used to be for me to do anything just for me. In the past I had given in to the wants and needs of others, and put myself at the back of the line. Now, several years later, I made choices on my behalf, gave up a lot of "shoulds" and seldom felt guilt.

Strangely enough, while I thought about the guilt peacemakers often experience — since we're doing something different, not something wrong — the chairperson of the meeting suggested that we talk about guilt.

Polly's effervescent, extroverted personality, which her recovery process was helping her to reclaim, made her one of the first to share. She said she was trying to accept the fact that her daughter's anorexia was not her fault. However, she still felt guilty when she saw Annie pushing food around on her plate. She admitted that she still wanted to fix Annie, and she got mad at her husband when he tried to force Annie to eat. She clenched her fists and said, "He makes her sit at the table, until she's cleaned her plate. She's eighteen, not eight. I don't think he learned anything at New Beginnings. I've tried to talk to him. But he won't listen . . ." Then, she asked for feedback from the group.

A woman slightly older than Polly shared next. She said she faced similar circumstances when her son was a teenager. She said her husband criticized his clothes, his friends, his grades, even the way he walked. She said both her husband and son tried to get her to take sides, and she bounced back and forth between them like a beach ball, until a counselor told her to get herself out of the middle by insisting that they speak to each other and not through her.

At meetings, I tried not to share things I learned in college. I didn't say that counselors used the word "triangulation" to describe this kind of interaction. It was an easy word for me to remember, since it rhymes with strangulation, and I'd been in the middle where I felt like I was being strangled. I myself got out of the way when one of my counselors explained that every child yearns to have a relationship with both of his parents, and every time I tried to smooth things over, I was robbing my sons of an opportunity to work out their differences with their father.

I glanced at Polly to see her expression. She was frowning, probably because she was again being told to let go, not what she wanted to hear.

Another group member recommended that she read a poem called "Children" from the book *The Prophet* by Kahlil Gibran. She said she put a copy of this poem on her refrigerator and read it daily when her kids were teenagers; it helped her to feel better, less responsible for some of the things they did.

Polly spoke again, changing the subject. While she was obviously struggling to find the serenity to accept the things she could not change, she lifted her spirit by focusing on something she was changing. She said she had rejoined Weight Watchers, this time to please herself, not Ty. She explained the new Weight Watchers program, saying she could eat whatever she wanted. In the new system each food had a point value assigned to it, and she could eat twenty-five points a day. She thought of the points as dollars and tried to spend them on fruits, vegetables, whole grains, fish and lean meets, which she ate in small portions at regular intervals throughout the day. At the end of the day, if she had points left over, she sometimes rewarded herself with a small treat. As a result of this effort, she had lost five pounds in the first month. Members of the group applauded her success.

Polly went on to say that she wanted to be a good role model for Annie, something she was not when Annie was growing up, something she felt guilty about, but at least she was trying to change. She claimed that her involvement in Annie's treatment helped her understand her own eating disorder, one that she'd developed when she was a child and her parents made her eat everything on her plate and rewarded her with dessert.

Recently, she learned that she had to change the way she thought about food if she wanted to be permanently slender. She had come to be fascinated by the similarities between Annie and herself, and their struggles with food. While her subconscious mind made her feel better about herself, if she finished everything on her plate. Annie had programmed her subconscious mind to believe that starving herself dissolved her difficulties.

"And," Polly claimed, "Annie and I both have to learn how to stand up to Ty, if we want to recover from our eating disorders! I can no longer use food to force my feelings down, and Annie will feel like she has control over more than her weight, if she learns to speak for herself."

I wanted to yell, "Hooray!" Polly got it. Many clients and family members finished our program, and I couldn't tell if they understood what we tried to teach them. Hearing Polly share made me know that at least one of our participants was changing for the better.

A long time ago, one of my mentors told me to seize every opportunity to work with mothers. He said, "If you help the mother, you help the whole family." Maybe he was right. Watching Polly give up her peace-at-any-price philosophy and take charge of her well-being helped me to feel optimistic about her and Annie.

The last person to share something about himself at this meeting was an obese, thirty-something man. He said that one of the things on his laundry list of character defects was, "We get guilt feelings when we stand up for ourselves." It seems he'd been telling his wife how he felt when she yelled at him, something he didn't do before coming to these meetings, since standing up for himself made him feel guilty. He expressed gratitude for continuing to use assertiveness skills with her; he didn't feel guilty now, and his new skills were increasing his self-esteem and helping him to lose weight. He admitted, though, that he still had a lot of weight to lose, but he sounded enthusiastic about the changes he'd made.

Having a Resentment Is Like Wetting Your Pants. Everyone Can See It and You're the Only One Who Can Feel It

On my way home from the meeting, I silently gave thanks for the blessings that had come into my life since I had begun my recovery process. Mostly, I felt grateful for getting rid of my fear of anger, my resentments, and the guilt feelings that had made it impossible for me to enjoy life. Overcoming these crippling emotions was a process, not something I did in a short amount of time. Some of my therapy sessions were largely responsible for my release from these emotions.

The session that stands out most in my mind — one I will never forget — is when my therapist asked me to picture my father in an empty chair and tell him exactly how I felt when I was a child.

When I said, "Dad," I started to cry. In between sobs, and the time it took for me to catch my breath, I said, "You were terrible. I was afraid of you. Every time I saw your truck in the driveway, I felt scared and angry. I knew you'd pick a fight with Mom, and we'd either run for our lives or stay, and she'd get hurt. I watched you hit her. I begged you to stop. Sometimes, when you were home, I tried to stay awake all night, so that I could break up a fight. If I fell asleep and the next morning I saw Mom wearing sunglasses to hide a black eye, I felt guilty. I blamed myself because sometimes I got between you and Mom, and I stopped you. Now I know it was not my fault. You were wrong. You had no right to hit her."

When I was done having my say, actually putting into words the feelings I'd kept inside for more than thirty years, a peaceful feeling enveloped me. It was unlike anything I'd ever experienced. I felt relaxed and confident. The war I had waged inside myself was over. By speaking my truth aloud, I was able to let go of the resentment I felt towards my father and forgive myself for the times I failed to protect my mother.

What happened a few months later was greater proof of how performing that simple, five-minute therapeutic exercise had the power to heal. I saw an ad on TV for Louis L'Amour books on tape. When my father was "on the wagon," he read all of L'Amour's western novels. Immediately, I said to myself, "I wish Dad was alive, so that I could buy him those tapes"; and I found profound surprise in those words.

My feelings toward my father had changed. I actually wanted to do something nice for him. Then, I remembered the past — how I dreaded the task of picking out birthday and Father's Day cards. My stomach churned and my heart beat faster when I saw cards that said, "You Are a Wonderful Father" or "You Were Always There for Me." Frantically, I would search for a card that carried little or no sentiment and felt relieved when the ordeal of buying a card for Dad was over. I hoped that my feelings toward him would change when he died. They didn't.

When I bought flowers for his funeral, I was a dutiful daughter fulfilling my obligation, nothing more. But after I had my say, got it all out in the open, my feelings changed. For the first time in my life, I was at peace with my past, and I wanted to give my father a gift.

From then on, I saw my father in a different light. The mean, terrible things he did, while under the influence of alcohol, faded from my memory. In place of some of those fearful memories came thoughts of kind deeds. One of my favorite memories of my father begins with me waking up in the wee hours of a wintry morning . . .

I look out my upstairs bedroom window and notice the snow on top of our car, which tells me that several inches of snow have fallen while I slept. I turn on the radio. Keeping the volume low, I listen to find out if school is closed for a snow day. When several schools in the area are mentioned and my school is not, I again look out my bedroom window. I make note of how much snow is on the road, and in my mind I argue with our principal, who is always the last in the county to give us a day off. Suddenly, my attention shifts. I see someone shoveling our neighbor's driveway. It seems strange for anyone to be shoveling; it's still dark out. Beneath the street light, I can see that the man shoveling is wearing a black-and-red hunting cap pulled down over his ears, just like the one my father wears. Then, I realize that the man I'm looking at is my dad. I continue to watch him as he finishes one driveway and moves on to the next. Before dawn, he removes the snow from three of our neighbor's driveways!

I never heard my father speak of his good deeds. Being able to do something nice for people he barely knew must have been all the reward he needed.

The rewards I received for allowing myself to speak the truth about what happened when I was a young, defenseless child are enormous. I can still remember how my father behaved when he was drunk. But the emotional charge that accompanied those thoughts has disappeared. In fact, at times, it feels like my childhood happened to someone else. I am not weighted down with resentments and stuffed full of guilt. The therapy I was privileged to experience made it possible for me to forgive my father and release me from my past. It helped me know what I'm responsible for and what I'm not. Consequently, my subconscious mind, which houses my feelings, makes me feel guilty only when I've done something wrong.

REFLECTIONS

1. Write about what makes you feel guilty.

2. Are you feeling guilty because you're saying or doing something wrong? Or are you feeling guilty because you're behaving differently?

3. Do you have any resentments? If you answer, "Yes," are you willing to have your say, get it all out so you can let go of this person and the emotions that are harming you?

Chapter 6

Any Time We Blame Someone or Something, We Give Our Power Away

At New Beginnings, Alumni Week was the best week of the year. Graduates of our Eating Disorder Program arrived from every state on the eastern seaboard and Canada. They came with suitcases full of smaller sizes, an article of clothing that showed how big they used to be, before and after snapshots, new hairdos and makeup. They screamed with delight when they could and could not recognize each other.

The 30 days they had spent together, at least one year ago and up to two, had created a closeness between them that was unlike anything they'd ever experienced. During their daily group therapy sessions, they shared things about themselves that they'd never said aloud. Their true confessions made them remove their masks and purge the pain from their past. The self-disclosures of one patient inspired another and then another to tell their secrets. In doing this, they were able to give and receive the unconditional love that the human spirit wants and usually does not ask for. They were among the few on this planet who had gone through a process that made them comfortable with everything that had happened to them and all their emotions. They no longer felt uncomfortable and wanted to change the subject when someone broke societies "don't-talk" and "don't-feel" rules.

In addition to learning to love themselves and others more, their recovery process allowed them to receive the blessings of true forgiveness. By sharing their deepest wounds, they were forced to feel the depth of the emotions they'd stuffed and let them go. They learned first hand that the way out of any emotional struggle is through it. For years, prior to treatment, they held onto their pain, the enemy within that stole their serenity and zapped their strength, since they didn't know how to get rid of it.

The enormous amount of weight they lost was a symbol of the emotional baggage they'd unloaded. Together they had done what they could not do alone. Consequently, they were eager to get back together with some of their best friends. Some of them had kept in touch. All of them, at least 10 women for every man, were excited about a week long reunion.

They spent the first day taking care of their physical needs. Besides finding their rooms and putting belongings away, they met with our nutritionist who updated their individual food plans in accordance with the amount of weight they'd lost.

On the second day, Connie gave her talk on co-dependency. Because she'd given the same scintillating speech for several years, word-of-mouth advertising packed the conference room with over 100 food addicts and staff members. We were probably in violation of the fire code; at least 20 of us were standing.

Much has been written about co-dependency, yet most people still have trouble understanding what it means. Many of us tend toward black-and-white thinking; therefore, we don't know the difference between a co-dependent or a peace-at-any-price person and someone who's just nice.

I recall a time when I was carrying my lunch tray back to my office. I asked one of our patients to open the cafeteria door for me. She said, "No, you're not going to catch me being co-dependent." I then asked another patient, who was willing to risk getting tagged with the label because she knew I wasn't trying to trick her and really needed help. The incident made me laugh and know that some of our patients still needed more information on this subject.

When we are children, long before we use any substance or activity to soothe ourselves, we interact with the significant people in our lives. Unfortunately, many of us are forced to deal with a parent who yells, sulks, uses threats or violence to express themselves. Naturally, we find ways to protect ourselves from them. A common defense is to become a peace-at-any-price person. We don't want to say or do anything to upset them. Therefore, we stop making decisions, try to control things that are beyond our control and hold on tight to whoever or whatever makes us feel safe.

Connie's audience recognized these traits in themselves when she told the following jokes and story. First she asked, "Does anyone know what the co-dependent said when the cab driver asked her where she wanted to go?" A male member of the audience yelled, "Wherever you're going will be fine." We laughed.

Next Connie told a story about herself asking a friend if she was going to have an alcoholic beverage on a flight they were taking together. Her friend exclaimed, "Drink — on an airplane! Are you crazy? What if the pilot needs help?" She had to wait for what seemed like a long time for everyone to stop laughing.

Connie followed these poignant punch lines by advising us to take a co-dependent with us if we go mountain climbing, since that person would hang on to the ends of the lines and never let go. Again, the joke gave us a good look and laugh at ourselves.

After educating, entertaining and warming up her audience for at least 30 minutes, Connie quoted the following lines she'd taken from an off-Broadway musical by Nancy Ford and Gretchen Cryer, titled, *I'm Getting My Act Together and Taking It On The Road*:

"All those years you were living with someone who was hiding behind a smile.

"All those years I was someone else, deception was my style.

"I closed you out by asking for nothing because I needed someone to blame.

"You couldn't give what I didn't ask for. It was a perfect game."

The room was quiet. Members of the audience looked at the floor or stared off into space. Some of them crossed their chests with their arms; others put their hands in their pockets. Tears slid down the cheeks of a few.

After a 15-minute break, reunion participants went into smaller group rooms for a therapy group called, "Relationships in Recovery." To keep the groups small enough to give everyone a chance to share, every counselor on staff facilitated a group.

As you might expect, alumni who returned for the reunion were the ones who had lost a lot of weight and kept it off. To do this, they had eliminated sugar and white flour — their drugs of choice — from their diets. Because they had stopped using food the way an alcoholic uses alcohol, they were more in touch with their feelings than ever before. They had stopped relying on food to medicate themselves. Consequently, they were less attracted to their spouses who were still using food, alcohol, drugs, work, over-spending, sex, exercise or always keeping busy to anesthetize themselves. Prior to recovery, many of them had unspoken pacts with their spouses, such as, "I won't mention your drinking, if you ignore my weight." Now they were vigilant about what they put into their mouths and less willing to overlook their partners' compulsive behaviors.

The words "in sickness and in health" took on new meaning for them. Now they were learning that when it comes to addictions, like attracts like. They were looking back at the person they used to be and realizing that their obsession with food was a secret that kept them in sickness and attracted them to a mate who was also trying to hide his or her compulsion.

There were eight people in the group I led, and all but one of them expressed some kind of dissatisfaction with their partner. Most of them prefaced what they really wanted to say with things like "He's a good father, provider, nice guy." We waited for the inevitable "but." The most common complaints were "He drinks too much"; "He won't talk to me"; "We don't have sex"; "I feel lonely"; "All he does is work"; and "He's fat."

The last woman who shared her marital problems admitted that she constantly thought about getting a divorce and felt guilty. She said she knew she was to blame; she was the one who had changed.

I asked her how much weight she'd lost. She said, "Sixty-eight pounds." I asked her if her weight loss affected her health. She replied, "Oh, yes. Now I'm only borderline diabetic, so I don't have to take insulin. My blood pressure is normal, and my cholesterol has come way down. My lower back, knees and feet don't hurt; I'm getting around better and enjoying life again."

"Are you going to fault yourself for making these changes?" I asked.

"No, but it's affected my marriage, and now I don't know what to do."

"You don't know what to do about what?" I asked.

"Should I stay with him or leave him?"

"I think you've forgotten some of the important tools of recovery," I told her. "Can anyone tell her what they are?" I glanced around at the other members of the group and waited.

Josh raised his hand, saying, "You need to live in the now and use assertiveness skills. When your husband says or does something that offends you, you need to tell him what he did, how you felt and ask for what you want. And you need to stop torturing yourself with the stay-or-leave decision that you're obviously not ready to make. Leaving is like getting a haircut. You know you're ready when you can't stand it another day. I know. I've been there. And I couldn't leave until I was ready to leave. Then, I couldn't stay another minute."

I watched the group members. They nodded and smiled at Josh's comforting words of wisdom. A few of them breathed a sigh of relief. We all felt better. Group work is gratifying when a member says exactly what needs to be heard. And I must admit that I sometimes forget to use assertiveness skills and live just for the moment. I appreciated Josh's words as well.

Growth Continues When Blame Is Gone

I took the last few minutes of group time to explain the negative power of blame. In addition to using assertiveness skills to take care of their emotional selves and living in the now, I wanted them to stop blaming anyone or anything. I asked them to think about what they sometimes blame when they're unhappy. I admitted that I used to get mad at the weather when I lived up north and blamed it for all my problems. I said, "I can't enjoy life. It's cold out!" By doing this, I was giving my power to the weather, something I couldn't control.

One group member said her father was an alcoholic, and she realized that she used him as her excuse, her scapegoat. Why? She wasn't ready to own responsibility for her unhappiness. She still needed someone to blame; so she married an alcoholic. She made us laugh when she said, "You don't have to wait long for an alcoholic to screw up and give you an excuse to be miserable!"

Besides their spouses, group members identified God, fate, the devil, luck, their Zodiac sign, their past, parents and kids as what they blamed. One lady admitted that she had to find something else to blame; she used to think her weight was her only problem. I watched many group members nod their heads in agreement with what she said.

I thanked them for their honest insights and sharing, and reminded them that their lives could be full of love, peace and joy — if they refused to give their power away by blaming anyone or anything. I asked them to keep in mind that people and things only have as much power over us as we give them. Lastly, I recommended that they ask themselves what their payoff could be if they didn't resist the temptation to give their power away by blaming.

REFLECTIONS

1.   Are you blaming anyone or anything?

2.   Are you willing to take back your power by refusing to blame?

Chapter 7

Sometimes We Have to Surrender to Win

This week I met with the father of a musically talented son who complained that his son does not enjoy football. I spent a 50-minute session with a 42-year-old mother who's still looking for a way to make her own mother notice her. And I listened to a wife say she walks on egg shells, always gives in to her husband, does everything she can think of to keep the peace, and he still flies off the handle over the least little thing.

The majority of my practice is made up of people who are wasting precious moments of their lives trying to change people and situations that are beyond their control. Some of them take prescribed drugs to lessen their feelings of hopelessness, worthlessness and anxiety. All of them benefit, if they learn what they can and cannot control.

While working with them, I frequently remind myself of my B.C. years. B.C. stands for Before Control because prior to going to support groups and therapy, all I had was an illusion of control. What I could control — myself — was out of control. I frequently felt frustrated, acted annoyed and surrendered my serenity.

Al-Anon and meetings for Adult Children of Alcoholics and Other Kinds of Dysfunctional Families taught me not to go in to my head alone. It was a dangerous place for me to be. To help me stay out of my hazardous head, they taught me slogans. In addition to the often repeated and printed on t-shirts and bumper stickers, "One Day At A Time," "Easy Does it" and "First Things First," my favorite is "Sometimes You Have To Surrender To Win."

While growing up in a family that was devastated by domestic violence, I learned to hate my father's anger and fear my mother's sorrow. Consequently, when I married, I took on the challenge of making everyone in my family happy and peaceful. To do this, I tried to stop them from expressing what they felt and gave them solutions to their problems. If my son complained about a playmate, I told him to play with someone else. If my husband squawked about his boss, I told him to get a new job. They could all depend on me to try to fix their feelings with sensible solutions.

Doing this came naturally to me. My subconscious mind holds my scary childhood memories, and it automatically pushes me toward pleasure and away from pain. Therefore, this part of my mind that controls over 90 percent of what I do tried to protect me from what I feared most — painful emotions. It believed it could fix feelings — mine and my loved ones. I didn't know that feelings don't obey commands or respond to "shoulds." They are not right or wrong. They just are, and as long as we're alive, we'll have them. And the best way to make peace with our feelings is to be honest about them.

I didn't have many friends or associates. Trying to do the impossible for four people — one husband, two kids and myself — was exhausting. I chose not to have a social life because I didn't want to try to fix feelings for anyone besides the members of my immediate family.

Living in isolation gave me abundant time and energy to spend on my family. I wanted to be an exceptional parent more than anything else, and I thought I was just that, until my sons were teenagers. Then, they acted out the emotions they were not allowed to express. Their sibling squabbles soared, their grades dropped and most of the time they looked unhappy.

My desire to be an exceptionally good parent led me to a Parent Effectiveness Training (PET) class. The PET teacher said children feel valued by parents who are empathetic, and they learn to feel good about themselves, if they were allowed to express their feelings and solve their problems. She said children who learn to solve little problems when they're small are better prepared to handle bigger problems when they grow up.

Each week parents in the PET class told stories about how they were interacting differently with their kids. They looked proud when they announced that they had stopped trying to control their children's feelings; and they waited patiently for their children to solve their own problems.

While I was taking the course, my oldest son, Nathan, was not getting along with his girlfriend. He acted out his discomfort by picking more fights than usual with his brother, and he gave me curt responses when I reminded him to do his chores. In my attempt to be like the parents in my class, I asked Nathan if he wanted to talk with me about his girlfriend.

He response was a firm, "No!"

"Cheer up," I said. "You're young. There are lots of fish in the sea."

He went to his room and slammed the door behind him.

I didn't feel good about what I said to him. But I was tired of watching him mope around the house. Besides, what I said was true.

Rationalizing my response didn't help. I felt guilty. I decided not to tell my PET classmates about my interaction with my son. A couple of weeks later, I dropped out. I justified my decision by telling myself that I'd have to be a saint to do all the PET class recommended.

Shortly thereafter, I agreed to participate in an intensive outpatient therapy group for Adult Children of Alcoholics and Other Kinds of Dysfunctional families. Participating in this group taught me why it was difficult for me to be empathetic to my children's feelings. I was not sensitive to their feelings because I was insensitive to my own. I was raised by troubled parents who taught me to obey the "don't-feel" rule. My father often said, "If you're going to cry, I'll give you something to cry about." One of my mother's favorite expressions was, "Smile and the world smiles with you. Cry and you cry alone." Consequently, I stuffed my feelings and taught my sons to swallow theirs.

Therapy put me in touch with the feelings I'd suppressed. It taught me that the way *out* of emotional pain is *through* it. After I purged the pain from my past, I was more comfortable with the honest expression of feelings, mine and my children's.

Therapy also taught me that growing up in an alcoholic family gave me an intense need for control. When I was a child, I never knew what was going to happen next. Dad might start yelling and embarrass me. Or he might come home drunk and hit Mom. Because I didn't want to experience anything similar to my childhood, I was desperate in my attempt to make my husband and children happy.

My need for control was natural due to the environment I survived as a child. However, it caused me to infect my sons with low self-esteem. Every time I told them what I thought they should do to solve their problems, I was indirectly saying, "You're inadequate. You need me to tell you what to do."

Discovering that I was an insensitive mother with an intense need for control who had unknowingly hurt my kids was painful. I was not the good mother I wanted to be. Gradually, I accepted this truth about myself. I knew I had to become a better parent.

By the time I realized that I'd passed my low self-esteem onto my kids by giving them advice instead of empathy, they were teenagers. I was afraid there was nothing I could do to erase my mistakes. I tortured myself with "if onlys." If only I'd had therapy before they were born. If only I'd know then what I know now.

While I was chastising myself for being a bad mother, I noticed that I hadn't seen Nathan's girlfriend for a while and asked him if he was still dating her.

His response, "I've said good riddance to bad rubbish."

"I'll bet you have reason to be angry at her," I said.

He looked surprised. "I treated her right. She's dating a guy with a bad reputation. I can't figure out girls. They drop nice guys to date losers."

"How unfair," I said.

Again, he gave me a surprised look. "I'm going to give my time and attention to earning money for a car, until someone who appreciates me comes along. I'm not going to waste anymore time or money on girls like her!"

"It sounds like you're making a good decision for yourself," I said.

He smiled and kissed my cheek. "Thanks, Mom. You're the greatest."

And I felt great. It wasn't too late for me to be empathetic and stop giving advice. And it wasn't too late for my sons to have a positive response to my empathy.

I Am The Only Person I Can Change

By changing myself, no one else, I changed all of my relationships. By simply responding differently to everyone, even the most difficult personalities, the ones who knew me best and therefore knew which buttons to push, I improved all of my relationships. Granted, many of them still did not do what I wanted them to do. But in time, as I continued to focus only on my words and actions, their responses did not bother me because I felt better about myself and was more relaxed. I wasn't trying to do the impossible. Finally, I had found the peace for which I'd been looking.

The people I met and the true stories I heard at support group meetings made it possible for me to hold onto my new way of life. Their honest self-disclosures kept me mindful of the futility of trying to change anyone but myself.

One of the best tales came from a recovering alcoholic, a former troublemaker. He said he went to a bar every day after work. After he'd downed a few drafts, he started to feel guilty about the time he spent away from his family and the chores he left undone. He told his drinking buddies to save his place at the bar. He went home, picked a fight with his wife and returned to the reserved bar stool, feeling angry and justified, but not guilty. He rationalized his daily drinking by telling himself that anyone who was married to his wife would drink. Years later, his wife attended Al-Anon and learned that she had to surrender to win. From then on, when he came home looking for a fight, she didn't give him what he wanted. She smiled at him, refused to argue and thereby let him keep his uncomfortable guilt feelings. For a few months he went back to the bar, the beer and his buddies. But eventually he decided to get rid of the unbearable guilt feelings by going to AA and acknowledging his powerlessness over alcohol. He surrendered. He won. Today he gives thanks for a good marriage, healthy, well-mannered adult children and financial abundance, rewards he and his wife have received since she stopped trying to control him and he stopped trying to control his drinking. Their peaceful expressions and hearty laughs convince me that they've found life's best rewards.

REFLECTIONS

1. Write down as many things as you can think of that are beyond your control.

2. What relationships can you improve by changing the way you interact within the relationship?

Chapter 8

We Treat Ourselves the Way We Were Treated

The subconscious mind, which holds our memories and feelings, has the power to protect and to haunt us. It protects us by automatically pushing us toward pleasure and away from pain. This explains why people who associate food with pleasure head for the refrigerator when they're upset. By understanding how our subconscious mind works, we can also appreciate how hard it is for someone who connects smoking with "fitting in" to quit.

The subconscious does not judge or discern. It simply compels us to want what's felt good in the past and to avoid who and what caused us pain. The memories and the feelings housed in our subconscious minds do not change, unless we become conscious of them and make an effort to change them. Even then, the task of changing what controls over 90 percent of what we habitually do is difficult.

Both our miserable and merry memories are embedded in our subconscious mind. They spill out to elate or haunt us when something in our environment reminds us of them. This explains why many of us dread the holidays and feel relieved when they're over. Holiday decorations, music, cooler temperatures and festive foods bombard our senses and trigger our subconscious to bring forth memories of Christmas' past. If we tried to bury our past like Ebenezer Scrooge in *A Christmas Carol*, the things we associate with the holiday season remind us of what we've tried to forget and make us feel depressed.

Everything from the star on the top of the tree to the smell of turkey cooking and the sound of Bing Crosby's voice singing carols remind us of the losses and traumas we've repressed. And, to make matters worse, while we're keeping busy or using a substance to distance us from our emotions, we're constantly being told to "be merry" and to "have a happy holiday." Because we cannot lift our spirits the way we light our tree — with the flick of a switch — these fair-thee-well wishes make us wonder what's wrong with us.

The only way out of emotional pain is through it. Unfortunately, we live in a society that does not encourage us to purge our pain. Small children instinctively and rapidly heal their hearts by expressing emotions. While we're growing up, we learn society's dysfunctional rules and start to deny and avoid our feelings and lose the happy person we were born to be. In other words, we learn to treat ourselves the way we were treated.

My father's birthday was December 24th. Even during the best of years, when he quit drinking for six months or more, he always "fell off the wagon" in time to celebrate his birthday. Prior to beginning therapy at the age of 37, I hadn't allowed myself to revisit the horrible holidays of my childhood. Instead of dealing directly with the terrible traumas caused by domestic violence, I became an escape artist. I found that exercising enough to exhaust myself and always keeping busy helped me to medicate my emotions. When sights, sounds, smells and tastes of the holiday season triggered my memories, the coping skills I used to alleviate my pain throughout the rest of the year let me down. I was quick to lose my temper, often fought back tears, and felt relieved and grateful when I took the tree down.

Fortunately, I chose a field of study that forced me to deal with my past. During my final internship, while working in a treatment center, a deep sadness enveloped me one evening while I was Christmas shopping. To relieve my discomfort, I did what I'd always done. I counted my blessings. At a time when many people were out of work, I reminded myself how lucky I was to have a job and enough money to spend on gifts for loved ones. Suddenly, I realized that I was doing to myself what I asked my clients not to do — deny their feelings.

Feeling like a hypocrite made me stop shopping, go home and allow myself to remember what happened, how I felt when I was a kid and have a good cry. Alone, wrapped in a blanket and hugging a teddy bear, I dropped my defenses and permitted the memories living in my subconscious mind to come forth, so that I could grieve them. This simple, completely normal way to deal with feelings made it possible for me to let go of my past, move on, be merry and have a "happy holiday season." The seasonal sorrow that had haunted my holidays has not returned.

It's Hard to See The Picture When You're In the Frame

After I broke the "don't-talk" and "don't-feel" rules, I felt sorry for my paternal grandmother, Gramma Day. Before Freud began his work in Vienna, the little girl who became my grandmother, Johanna Lievense, was traumatized by her mother's murder. While Freud was identifying defense mechanisms, Johanna had nothing to relieve her emotional pain, except her defense mechanisms. Evidence of the strong, unresolved, secretive feelings she had about her trauma and loss come from the fact that she avoided the topic by switching from English to Dutch every time someone mentioned her past.

Knowing that our subconscious minds are programmed by repetition and the intensity of our experiences, I decided to find out how my great grandmother was killed and if Gramma Day was present when her mother was murdered. Luckily, before I saved the money I needed to travel abroad, I was introduced to a type of computer software that assisted me with my search. While looking for this information, I fought off my fear of records being lost during World War II or "The Great Disaster," a name the Dutch had given to a 1953 flood that killed more of them than World War II. A reminder to myself that the Dutch were known to be good record keepers and that Anne Frank's diary survived kept me going.

I referred to the letter I had received from my cousin Jane, as well. It supplied me with the information I required to get started.

The first record I attained was a copy of a passenger list with the name Johanna Lievense. The list showed that she departed from Rotterdam, a port in southern Holland, to Ellis Island in this country on February 15, 1892.

Next I found a Holland website, www.zeeuwarchief.n. Email communication with this site let me know that they would search the data I provided for a reasonable fee. A few months later I received the following letter.

Uw brief:E-mails Dec. 3 2001
Uw kenmark:
Ons kenmerk:
Onderwerp:murder Adriana Lievense
Bijlage:
Middleburg, February 1, 2002

Dear Mrs. Poor,

I am worry that it took so long to answer your e-mail but due to illness and holidays of my colleagues you had to wait a little longer. However the results of my investigation will surely satisfy you !

Worker Izaak Timmerman, living in Oostburg, had been in jail several times for acts of violence. In February 1875 he was a member of a group persons who molested someone. He was caught by the police and condemned to eight months jail. In the afternoon of 11 October 1876 he was in the house of Johannes Timmerman in Oostburg and had a terrible quarrel with his wife Adriana Lievensse. The furniture was broken to pieces. Again he had drunk too much and lost control. In the corridor he cut her throat. Adriana, 31 years old, born in Hoofdplaat as a daughter of Thomas Lievensse and Sara van Hoeve, died that day, about 17.00 h (see copy). The newspaper Terneuzensche courant of 14 oct. 1876 tells us that the neighbour's wife took their only child out of the house when the crime was just committed. The murderer was immediately arrested by the 'Marechaussee' (military police) and brought to prison. He confessed at once. The paper mentions that Isaac Timmerman spent several times in jail after he was dismissed from the Army. He was known as a very bad and dangerous fellow. Due to the severity of the crime and the former crimes he had committed the lawcourt of Middelburg was not competent. Therefore he was brought to 's-Gravenhage (theHague) in January 1877 where the Court of Justice condemned him to 20 years House of Correction (see copy). It was proven that he killed his wife on purpose, but not proven that he already had plans to do so.

I have enclosed a page of the jailregister. (Register Ruis Arrest) in Middelburg. There you can find a description ('signalement') of Isaac Timmerman: son of Abraham Timmerman and Maria de Roo, born in Biervliet, living in Oostburg, 30 years old, labourer, protestant, length: 1,648 m, his face had a healthy colour, he had a low forehead, a sharp nose, a round chin and a normal mouth, blue eyes, light-brown eyebrows, blond hair, a light-brown beard and one special mark: a scratch on the right side of his nose. He had followed lower education (see copy).

Yours sincerely,
A.F. (Toon) Franken
medewerker afdeling Archieven & Collecties

The words "cut her throat" and "the small child was removed from the house immediately after the murder occurred" stuck with me. Again and again, the picture of a little girl holding a neighbor's hand, walking out of a house where her mother had been killed, made my head and shoulders shake.

What makes this horrendous crime all the more horrible is the fact that three-year-olds view themselves as the center of the universe. If they live in pleasant surroundings and everyone they love is happy, their self-esteem increases because they think they're responsible for the happiness. If, on the other hand, they're subjected to misery and madness, as my grandmother was, they feel responsible and ashamed of themselves. This shame and accompanying low self-esteem remain in the child's subconscious mind. Pretending that the event never happened by refusing to talk about it does not make it go away. The child's subconscious mind retains the trauma, the sorrow and the shame. If the tragic event is brought out in the open and someone assures the child that what happened was in no way her fault, she can allow herself to grieve, reprogram her subconscious and be healed.

Additional information I acquired about the Lievense family revealed that

Johanna lived with her mother's younger sister, Aunt Sarah, until she came to America. When Johanna was eight, Aunt Sarah got married and every year or two thereafter she gave birth. I think it's safe to assume that Johanna provided some of the care for her little cousins.

During my search, I contacted a few relatives and discovered that some of them also wanted to know how Adrianna was killed. All of them assured me that Isaac was not Johanna's father. None of them told me how they knew this for sure. Since we have no DNA evidence, I do not know who my great-grandfather was. Certainly, it may have been the murderer because court records state that he was married to Adrianna.

Gramma Day and I have more in common than our genes and cultural backgrounds. More significant than being members of the same family and living part of our lives in the same town is the fact that we were both subjected to domestic violence at ages when we believed we were the center of the universe and thereby felt responsible for what happened to our loved ones. Consequently, we became shame-based, externally focused, peace-at-any-price personalities who put the wants and needs of others way ahead of our own.

We sought geographical cures. She moved from Holland at 19 years, and I moved from my small hometown in upstate New York to New York City at age 18. Like her, I avoided talking about my past. Neither one of us had heard Yogi Bera's wisdom, "Wherever you go there are," so we carried on like nothing out of the ordinary had happened. We didn't know that the pain we buried affected the way we felt, the decisions we made and the lives we led.

I suspect that she agreed to marry Jacob, the last member of the Day family to leave home, to avoid small town, turn-of-the-century gossip and shame. I can imagine that her peace-at-any-price personality robbed her of her right to make decisions on her own behalf, and she was willing to do whatever she thought she had to do to avoid another person's wrath, including getting married.

Lucky for me, there was at least one major difference in our lives. My mother lived longer and modeled some good parenting skills. Unlike Gramma Day, I never bought either one of my sons a car, and I would not have rewarded reckless behavior by replacing one.

REFLECTIONS

1. In what ways are you treating yourself the way you were treated when you were a child?

2. Do you have past events in your life that you need to feel to heal and grieve to leave?

Chapter 9

The Truth Needs
No Defense

With no window in my office at New Beginnings, I often left the door to the hallway open when I did my paperwork. After attending a counseling session with Connie, Polly stuck her head in the office and said, "Hi." Watching her and others who've gone through our program change is the best perk of my profession, so I invited her to have a seat.

I was amazed at how different she looked from the last time I saw her. Then, she had three chins and wore loose fitting clothes to hide the roll around her middle and the size of her hips. The woman seated in my office had one chin and high cheekbones. She looked fit and trim in her sweater and slacks, no more than a few pounds overweight. More noticeable than her weight loss was the change in her demeanor. She held her head higher, made better eye contact, spoke slower and clearer. I noticed that she carried a spiral notebook, so I asked her if she was doing her assignments. She nodded and gave me a big, genuine smile, not the fake, hide-her-feelings kind that she used to wear.

"Anything you've written down that you want to share with me?" I asked.

"Sure," she said. "My journal is turning into a book."

Connie always encouraged her clients to do writing assignments. She said that a written course of action would make it easier for them to find their way to a new, better way of life, the way written directions help us find new locations. She said that the definition of insanity is doing the same thing over and over again, expecting different results, and the best way to stop repeating mistakes is to log actions and intentions. Their journals, logs, notebooks, diaries, whatever one wishes to call them, gave them "concrete copies" of where they'd been and where they wanted to go. If they "lost their way," all they had to do was refer to what they'd written, become conscious of their words and actions, and get back on course.

In addition to a written, daily record of the foods she ate, Polly pointed to a subtitle that read, "We're Not Responsible For What We Feel, But We Are Responsible For What We Do With Our Feelings." Underneath it in large print, she's written, "TYRONE." Next to his name were several entries.

"How much do you want me to share?" she asked.

I enjoyed her energy and the lift I received from knowing our program helped her, so I said, "Go for it."

"Well, I'm finally aware of the personality traits that my father and Ty have in common. I used to think they were different. Ty doesn't drink. But they're both manipulative, inconsistent, selfish and quick tempered. My father's drinking caused family problems, and Ty makes life difficult for us with his spending habits. I'm beginning to suspect that he keeps us in debt to make us feel dependent on him. I was working two jobs to pay off our debts, and he came home with an expensive new car. I gave up one of my jobs, and I'm doing what I can to separate our finances. Best of all, I'm standing up to him. See, I have my assertiveness words written down."

Polly pointed to these words in her journal. When you . . . I felt . . . and I wish . . . Obviously, Connie was helping her to be assertive by giving her key words to remember. Every time Ty or anyone else said or did something that offended Polly, she was supposed to take care of her emotional self by telling the person specifically what they said or did that offended her, how she felt, and tell them how she wanted to be treated from now on. Of course, using these skills did not guarantee that the other person would treat her differently, but by taking care of herself, by having her say she did not have to stuff her feelings, be crippled by resentments, and end up blowing up over something small and insignificant.

"So what did you say to Ty when he showed up with the new car?" I asked.

"At first I didn't say anything. I was stunned. He catches me off guard. But a couple of days later, when I got in touch with what I was feeling, I said, 'Ty, when you spend money that we don't have and put us further in debt, I feel angry, and I wish you were more considerate of my feelings.' I know he's not going to take the car back, and he's probably not going to change. But I, at least, feel better about myself when I stand up to him. Every time I speak my mind, I realize that I can make choices. For now, I'm choosing to stay with him. If nothing else, he's a good person for me to practice my assertiveness skills on. If I can be true to myself with Ty, I'll be able to take care of myself with anyone. I have a long-standing habit of giving in to him that I need to break. I'm grateful to you, to Connie, and the others at New Beginnings who've taught me this."

"Be sure to thank yourself," I said. "The world is full of teachers. It's willing students who make the difference. We couldn't teach you anything, if you were unwilling to learn."

She pointed to the name ANNIE, then flipped through several pages quickly to give me an idea of how much she'd written about her daughter. "See how many times I've written that I'm powerless over her and underlined it? It's so hard for me to watch her destroy herself."

"Did you tell Connie what you just said about Annie?"

"Yeah."

"What did she say?" I asked.

"Let me think. We just talked about this. Connie said I could change the way I view Annie. Instead of thinking of her as destroying herself, I could honor her process. Something like that. She said I could see her as going through what she needs to go through which is similar to my process. But to me what she's doing seems worse."

"A few seconds ago you thanked me for helping you. So you're obviously pleased with the changes you've made. Right?"

"Oh, yes, very much so."

"What made you willing to change yourself?" I asked.

"Annie's problem. Well, that's what brought me here. Then, I started listening, mostly because I wanted to help her, and gradually I learned that the best way to help Annie was to change myself, especially the way I interact with her father."

"And all of that has been a process. Correct? Not something you did overnight?"

"Right."

"Can you honor Annie's process?" I went on. "Can you realize that she needs time to sort out what she's heard and decide if the payoffs of recovery are worth giving up the anorexia that helped her to feel more in control and better about herself?"

"Actually, she has gained weight. But I think she's becoming bulimic. She doesn't eat with us. I find fast food wrappers in her car, and some of the cookies I buy for Ty and my son Sammy disappear. I remember what some of the bulimic girls in the family sessions I attended said about going to several fast food places in one night. They said they ate pizza at Pizza Hut and threw it up, then headed straight to McDonalds for burgers and fries, purged them, only to top that off with Dunkin Donuts, then get rid of them. Annie's been hanging out with one of those girls, and they're talking about moving in together. I get scared when I think about it."

"Do you remember what the addicts in the family program said that motivated them to get clean and sober?" I asked.

"They hit bottom. Then, they said they were sick and tired of living that way. They wanted to get rid of the consequences.

The same holds true for people with eating disorders. When Annie hits bottom, when she's motivated, she'll begin recovery, not until."

"How does she afford her binges?"

"She has a job. We don't give her money."

"Good," I said. "And moving out will give her more expenses and less money to waste on binging and purging. It might help her to hit bottom. In the meantime, you're doing your part by setting a better example for her, by helping her realize that people don't have to be too thin or too fat. Now she has a role model who eats right, one who uses food as nutrition, not as a drug to escape feeling."

"Speaking of kids," Polly said, "I'm having a problem with Sammy, my fourteen year old. Every day when he gets home from school, he tells me that I'm lazy. He says that I don't do anything. I tell him that I provide for all our needs by shopping, cooking, cleaning and doing laundry. Plus, I do most of the yard work, and I go to college as well. He still insists that I do nothing —"

"Polly," I interrupted. "The truth needs no defense. He's pushing your buttons, putting you on the defensive by accusing you of being lazy, something you know you're not. Stop defending yourself."

"But he won't stop. He doesn't hear what I'm saying."

"Do you watch football?" I asked.

"Sometimes, but not much."

"Which team is most likely to score points, the offense or defense?" I asked.

"The offense," Polly answered.

"Right. So your son has the ball. All you've done so far is play defense. Find a way to take the ball away from him. Put yourself in scoring position."

"How?"

"You'll figure it out."

"I'll try," she said.

"Trying is lying. Just do it!" I told her.

Polly laughed. She'd heard that phrase before from members on our staff.

I am starting to figure some things out," she said. "Writing in my journal, keeping my therapy sessions and talking to support-group friends is helping me to understand myself and my life. I've decided that I have some injured parts caused by bad experiences that I never talked about or grieved. I've given these parts Indian names like Running Scared, Abandoned Adolescent and Wounded Wife. Sometimes I can tell when they're running my life."

I wanted to hear more of what she had to say about her injured parts, because clients who couple what they've learned from others with what they're learning from inside themselves do best. But the light on my phone flashed, indicating that my scheduled client had arrived, so I put my curiosity on hold and said, "So long," to Polly.

REFLECTIONS

1.   List the names of anyone who you allow to put you on the defensive.

2.   On the back of a wallet-sized card, write down:

     When you _____.

     I felt _____.

     I wish _____.

Carry this card with you to remind you to use assertiveness skills to care
for your emotional self.

Chapter 10

It's Okay to Be Angry, But Not to Be Cruel

A mistake peace-at-any-price people make is assuming that everyone wants to be peaceful. This assumption makes them keep their opinions to themselves, give up their wants and needs, even compromise their values, morals and principles to get along with a troublemaker. All this is to no avail. Troublemakers are not interested in keeping the peace. And kowtowing to them makes them worse. They have no respect for the people they can take advantage of. The mere presence of such a person aggravates them.

Remember the guys I mentioned in the introduction, the ones in the treatment center who told me how easy it was for them to find their enablers? I learned a lot from them, probably much more than they learned from me.

Most importantly, I learned that these I-want-what-I-want-when-I-want-it troublemakers are scared. During my internship when I started working with alcoholics and drug addicts, they said they were scared, and I didn't believe them. It didn't make sense. These were people who'd been shot, cut, bruised, bloodied, hospitalized and jailed. They'd lived on the streets and in crack houses.

They survived by stealing from stores, other junkies, foes, friends and relatives. They constantly lived on the edge, running from the law and their families, always finding just enough money to feed their hunger and their habit. When I met them, they were in a treatment center, surrounded by peers who understood them. Their basic needs were met, and no one wanted to harm them. *What did they have to fear?* I wondered.

As I learned more about them and their addictions, I realized they feared what they'd used drugs to avoid: themselves — especially their feelings and other people. By using drugs, they anesthetized their feelings and distanced themselves from people who loved them. Because they did not love themselves, they could not take love in. They felt uncomfortable when anyone tried to get too close. Drugs and alcohol took away their fears. These substances, which — to my way of thinking — put them in harms way, provided their escape from the emotions they wanted to numb. After the drugs were out of their systems, they were scared to death.

One way for a peace-at-any-price person to understand the fear that is behind the anger a troublemaker expresses is to recall what happened when a reckless driver almost forced her to have a serious accident. After she regained control of her car, her hands stopped shaking and her heart slowed down, she got mad. Even a person who never swears finds vulgar words in her vocabulary when she's frightened. Troublemakers are scared all the time. To them, life feels out of control. They deliberately start arguments, so that they can divert their attention away from their uncomfortable fearful feelings by focusing on what they say makes them angry.

On the outside peace-at-any-price people and troublemakers look like opposites. She who is nice to everyone, and he who creates chaos appear to be an example of opposites being attracted to each other. But if we look more closely, we realize that they're an example of similar personalities being attracted to each other, since they're both fearful. She's afraid of anger and, therefore, allows troublemakers to control her. He's afraid of feeling, being fully human, so he keeps anyone from getting too close by expressing anger.

While the peacemakers' fears are evident to troublemakers, the reverse is not true. Peacemakers think troublemakers are bold, brazen and in control of any situation. They do not see the person behind the mask who expresses anger to avoid feeling gut-wrenching emotions like jealousy, hurt, rejection, sorrow and terror. By constantly finding someone or something to be upset about, he feels powerful and in control, not vulnerable.

Troublemakers confuse peacemakers because they are not angry about what they say they're angry about. A troublemaker complains about his boss, his spouse, his kids, the neighbors and "bastards" on the road. He constantly finds fault with everything they do. Like Scrooge, what he's really upset about are the losses he didn't grieve and the hurts he never mourned. Throughout his lifetime, he may have absorbed punitive punishments from a frustrated father, and/or ingested insults from an ignorant mother and/or consumed cruel comments from his peers. Consequently, he has a slush fund of unresolved feelings and an enormous fear of dealing with them in what he thinks is an unsafe society. After all, his society taught him to obey the don't-talk and don't-feel rules. Therefore, he doesn't know that he has to feel it to heal it and grieve it to leave it. Thus, he resorts to expressing anger to give himself some relief.

Fear Is The Dark Room Where Negativity Is Developed

If an addict stops using drugs and alcohol, and does not attend recovery meetings (AA, NA, CA), where he is given an opportunity to break society's dysfunctional rules, he will continue to feel scared, not be able to relax, and will use anger to express himself. In recovery circles, a person who does this is called a "dry drunk." At home, he's probably called worse names by those who think they have to put up with his rude remarks and tolerate his nasty negativity.

The spouse of a wet or a dry drunk specializes in ignoring her irritations, forgetting her frustrations, renouncing her rage and avoiding angry people. Doing this zaps her strength and puts her at a disadvantage with the troublemakers she's attracted to her. Troublemakers, on the other hand, use their anger to get what they want. Instead of being paralyzed by a fear of anger, they harness the energy one derives from feeling angry and use it to their advantage.

Because anger is an emotion, it does not obey commands or respond to shoulds. It will not magically disappear, if we tell it to go away. Consequently, peace-at-any-price people, who deny their angry feelings, allow their anger to ferment inside of them. It turns into sorrow which makes them feel hopeless and worthless, guilty and shameful. They have difficulty with concentrating and remembering. Thus, they are ill prepared to deal with anyone, much less a troublemaker.

The way out of the depressed state of mind they created by not acknowledging their anger, by always trying to keep the peace, is through it. They can cure themselves of depression caused by the anger they have swallowed, if they will admit what they feel and change everything they can change that upsets them.

Unfortunately, in a society that discourages the honest expression of all feelings, most peacemakers have to hit a bottom before they get the help they need. Far too many become Edith Bunker (from the '70s television show, *All in the Family*). They act like Edith, scurrying around, trying to please their Archie (Edith's husband in *All in the Family*). Every day they listen to his negative, insidious comments. By trying to reach their goal — creating peace with someone who prefers conflict — they exhaust themselves.

What happens to the peacemaker as a result of her daily interaction with a troublemaker is similar to what happens to a rock that's constantly being hit by a drop of water. Parts of herself are whittled away. Her high tolerance for emotional abuse, something she most likely learned in her family of origin, and the peace-at-any-price philosophy she adopted, makes her carry on as if nothing is happening. But she is acting out the feelings she doesn't talk about. She has found a more acceptable compulsion than drugs and alcohol, something she won't get arrested for — like overeating, overspending, being a martyr or a victim — to medicate her emotional pain. She may justify the way she deals with her unexpressed feeling by saying that she's not hurting anyone, except herself, as if that's okay. And it's not true. She is someone's daughter, sister, friend and/or mother. When she fails to take care of herself, she also hurts them.

Peace-at-any-price people find ways to get even. Often they don't admit it, even to themselves, the ways they strike back at their troublemakers. But the anger they constantly stuff gets expressed.

Some "peacemakers" are passive-aggressive. They do things like always show up late, forget to do what the troublemaker asks of them, wear clothes he despises, feign headaches in the bedroom and try to make him feel jealous. Other get-even responses include snide remarks, sarcastic jokes and indifferent responses directed at their troublemaker. She or he (not all peace-at-any-price people are females) may also be guilty of taking out their anger on innocent bystanders. Their stuffed anger spews forth like lava from a volcano over something as insignificant as a cat jumping onto a table.

A pay off peace-at-any-price people get for trying to keep the peace with a troublemaker is this: They don't have to look too closely at themselves. As long as all their thoughts and energies are being used to make a troublemaker happy, they don't have to take a personal inventory and make meaningful self–improvements. But like I said earlier:

If nothing changes, then nothing changes.

The so-called peacemaker and troublemaker will stay trapped in their tit-for-tat relationship, until one of them gives up their desire to change anyone but him/herself and creates change by changing the way he/she interacts with others.

It's Okay To Laugh At Myself, But Not When I need To Cry

There are five steps a peace-at-any-price person can take to make herself feel great. And to help him/her remember these steps, I use the word GREAT as an acronym. The first step, the G, is to *Grieve Her Past*. Peacemakers attract troublemakers to them with their eager-to-please personalities. They developed their personality in response to parents who with words and by example taught them not to express their feelings. Consequently, they have not grieved their losses. Instead of allowing themselves to go through the natural grief process every time they suffered a loss, they stuffed their feelings, and these feelings are still trapped in their subconscious minds.

One reason small children are happy is they have not yet learned society's don't-talk and don't-feel rules. If a sibling or playmate snatches their favorite toy, they instinctively react by screaming, crying and pointing to the coveted toy. They know what they want, and they're not afraid to express their feelings to get it. Moments later, the incident is forgotten, and the toddlers are playing together, as if the dispute never happened. I don't think anyone could explain the word "resentment" to a small child. They couldn't grasp its meaning; they're too busy living life to swallow anger and allow it to turn sour and ruin their fun.

Unfortunately, while they're growing up, with words and actions, adults teach them to deny, avoid and stuff their feelings, so they learn what it means to feel resentful.

A peace-at-any-price person who wants to feel GREAT must get over her resentments by allowing herself to have her feelings. She needs to revisit her past, the way Scrooge did in his nightmare, and allow herself to have honest to goodness childlike feelings. Most people find it easiest to do this by talking to a trained professional, someone who will encourage them to get it all out. A few lucky people have a friend or relative who can be their empathetic ear.

Getting through the grief process is difficult for people who want to protect their parents and think they're doing something wrong if they tell the truth. What they're doing in the here and now to themselves and innocent people by acting out the feelings they stuffed is much worse than doing a therapeutic exercise to manifest healing. Their parents never need to know what they said and cried about to heal themselves.

I have worked with clients who say they can't remember their childhoods. This means that they experienced traumatic events too scary to recall. If they will allow themselves to talk about unimportant things — the little things they remember — gradually they'll recall more significant events and find the strength they need to purge the pain from the past.

The trip back to yesteryear unfolds the way we peel an onion, one layer at a time. By talking about it and feeling the unresolved pain, a person grows stronger and realizes that they are no longer a child at anyone's mercy. Thus, the fears that are held within the subconscious minds are released, and one develops a more mature approach to living life.

It's important not to use your inability to remember as an excuse not to grieve your past; we do not have to consciously remember what happened to us to be adversely affected by it.

For years, I listened to some of my relatives say that I was a weird baby; I walked when I was one, and at the age of two, I went back to crawling. Thinking about the little me this way increased the shame I already felt as a result of growing up in an alcoholic family. Finally, at age 37, I started reading self-help books and learned that my behavior was an example of regression. Shortly thereafter, I found my father's World War II discharge papers; they revealed that he was waging a war with the enemy when I was one year old. By the time

I was two, he was home, and I suspect he was waging a war with my mother. I went back to crawling to protect myself in much the same way that he must have gotten close to the ground to protect himself from enemy fire.

By continuing to read self-help books, I learned that members of an alcoholic family have a proverbial elephant in their living room, a problem big enough to ruin every area of their life and they ignore its presence. They try to function, as if nothing out of the ordinary is happening. Consequently, my family did not acknowledge the connection between my behavior and the family violence that would naturally frighten a small child. Instead of admitting the real problem — what they desperately wanted to deny — they called me weird. My search taught me that I wasn't weird, just too young to ignore the "elephant" and too scared to stand up.

The fact that I couldn't consciously remember feeling scared enough to go back to crawling did not give me an immunity from the effects of family violence. I continued to be afraid of anger, until I talked and cried about what happened in our house. Then, my fear went away, and I no longer felt compelled to "keep the peace."

In addition to working with a therapist and attending a group for adult children of alcoholics, I pictured what I remembered about my childhood on a movie screen. I pretended that I was an adult in the theatre, watching a movie about my life as a kid. I cried because I felt sorry for the little girl who tried so hard to protect her mom from her dad. After that, I realized that no one has ever died from crying. However, many, many people die every day from drug overdoses, suicides and drunk driving accidents. What's behind their need to engage in these dangerous activities is their need to cry.

The R in GREAT stands for *Refuse to Blame*. If we blame, we give our power away. After a peace-at-any-price person has gotten it all out, voiced the anger and hurt she feels about everything she remembers that has happened to her, she needs to let it go. If she gets stuck in blame and thinks of herself as a victim, she will continue to suffer from depression. If, on the other hand, she accepts that she cannot change her past, that all she can do is change the way she views it and recognize that what she's been through has made her a stronger, more empathetic person, then she will free herself from the bondage of crippling emotions.

Knowing that people, places and things have only as much power as we give them helps us to let go of blame. Think about what you blame for your unhappiness and give it up. Refuse to let the scapegoat you've named and blamed steal another second of your life by releasing it now.

The E in GREAT stands for *Erect Boundaries*. Show me a person who does not allow herself to feel and express anger, and I'll show you a person who has no boundaries. If you are such a person, you might not know what a boundary is. Boundaries are the words and actions we use to set limits. At one time or another, just about everyone who's in our life has tried to push the limit. Peace-at-any-price people have been nudged, pushed, shoved, prodded and forced to give in, hand over, donate, contribute, furnish and supply more than their share. In other words, they've taught others to take advantage of them. If they want this to stop, they must get in touch with the normal God-given emotion called anger and use it to take care of themselves.

Anger can be used as a weapon or a tool. It's a weapon capable of destruction, if we try to ignore it, turn it inward and get depressed. It's a weapon, if it comes out sideways and makes us impatient, sarcastic, rude, cruel and negative. It's a tool, if we use it to stay in touch with our feelings and erect boundaries. In other words, we become like small children who know what they want and are not afraid to ask for it. It's a tool, if we accept that anger is a necessary emotion, and we naturally feel it in response to cruelty and unfair treatment.

The A in GREAT stands for *Assert Yourself*. True peacemakers use assertiveness skills. Instead of arguing with troublemakers (What a waste of time and energy that is!) or swallowing their feelings, they take care of their emotional self by telling others what they said or did that hurt their feelings, how they felt, and they ask them not to do it again. Their intent is not to change the other person but to care for themselves, so they are not paralyzed by fears or weighted down with resentments.

Peace-at-any-price people are not quick on their feet. Remember, we developed our personalities in response to living with aggressive people. Therefore, we automatically shut down when we sense someone is angry. If this angry person says something that hurts our feelings, we don't have to use assertiveness skills immediately. We can wait hours or days, until we get in touch with our feelings, then use the skills. There's nothing that says we can't have a delay. What's important is that we have our say, own our feelings (we don't say you made me feel, because no one has the power to make us feel anything) and ask for what we want. Using these skills becomes part of what we do to take care of ourselves

— like drinking lots of water, eating fruits and vegetables, exercising and making time to have fun and to sleep.

After you've done the first four steps, the final step, the T in GREAT comes naturally. It stands for *Take Risks*. Overcoming a fear of anger is a peace-at-any-price person's biggest obstacle. After she's proved to herself that she can do this by standing up to her troublemakers, she's ready to get on with her life. To be precise, after she's given up her impossible goals, always keeping the peace and pleasing everyone, she's freed up the time and energy she needs to get everything she wants from life. She is ready to make all her dreams come true. By standing up for herself and using her anger as a tool when necessary, she's done more than she ever thought possible. Hence, she's proud of herself and eager to take on new challenges. By grieving her past, taking responsibility for her life by using boundaries and assertiveness skills, she's let go of all her "baggage." There's nothing left to weigh her down. She'll look for new opportunities and the risks she needs to take to make her life the exciting adventure it was meant to be.

To review, a peace-at-any-price person who wants to feel GREAT will

Grieve the Past,
Refuse to Blame,
Erect Boundaries,
Assert Yourself, and
Take Risks.

REFLECTIONS

1. If you're a "peacemaker," what do you do with the anger you swallow?

2. Do you have symptoms of depression, such as feeling helpless, hopeless, or worthless; difficulty sleeping, concentrating or remembering: increased or decreased appetitie; or suicidal ideation?

3. If you were not trying to please anyone but yourself, what would you do differently?

Chapter 11

Love Is Action

Did you ever pick the petals off a posey while reciting, "He loves me. He loves me not"?

I discovered that I could always come out with the answer I wanted, "He loves me," by counting or discounting the stem. But my gut was never convinced that a flower, a Ouija board or a crystal ball told the truth. Deep inside, I knew that it's easy to believe what I wanted to believe, and I could use those things to get the answers I wanted.

Today I don't need anything outside myself to know who loves me and who loves me not. I can tell by the way they treat me. While I still believe in the chemistry between two people that creates an "in love" feeling, the best feeling in the world, but certainly not the only good feeling, I don't have to wonder if someone loves me. I know by his actions. If he shows up on time, does what he says he's going to do, uses good manners, is considerate of my wants and needs, refrains from being impatient, sarcastic and cruel, he's treating me lovingly. Naturally, doing the opposite tells me he doesn't love me, because love is a verb.

A mistake a peace-at-any-price person often makes is trying to figure out why someone who says he loves her treats her so poorly. She spends precious hours of her life dissecting her relationship and her lover's life, so she can come up with a reason for unacceptable behavior. The best answer she can attain is no more than an assumption, a logical guess as to why someone's words and actions are not what she wants them to be.

The very worst answer one can derive from "assuming" is an excuse. You might say he's impolite, inconsiderate and always out for himself, because he had a bad childhood. Or he changed for the worst after he suffered a tragic loss, as if he's the only one who's had losses, and he's, therefore, not responsible for his words and actions. If he's not responsible, then who is?

Instead of asking, "Why?" I think we need to focus on the "What?" and "How?" What is the troublemaker in your life doing that upsets you? How can you change your response, so he suffers the consequences of his behaviors and you do not? Remember, we can be part of the problem or part of the solution. We do not want to reward negative behavior in adults anymore than we want to give in to a toddler's temper tantrum and, thereby, encourage him to continue to stamp his feet to get what he wants.

Adults have fits, too. Some are not as obvious as a small child's. Adults use sulking, insults, threats and other fight-and-flight conduct to get their way. We so-called peacemakers can give in to them and encourage them to continue to behave poorly, or we can refuse to reward negative behavior. The choice is ours.

Feelings Are not Facts

The thought of changing the way you react to a troublemaker might scare you. If you've been trying to keep the peace with an aggressive person for a long time, doing something new, like standing up to him, probably frightens you. You may think the worst will happen, if you have your say and refuse to give in to his unreasonable demands. If this is true, you are allowing your fear of the unknown to dictate your words and actions. But great feats and great relationships are not created by the power of fear.

I used to teach small children how to swim. On the first day of class, most of them walked through the gate to my backyard pool, clutching their towels to their chests. Some of them gave me interesting reasons for why they couldn't get wet, such as, "Mommy told me not to." I tried to make the lessons fun to distract them from their fears. I would first get them into the pool. Soon thereafter I got their heads wet, and before three weeks were up, I had them jumping off the diving board into deep water and swimming a few feet to the side of the pool.

Each new step was a scary step for them. Fortunately, every small class had one child who was a little more daring than the others. After he submerged his head, his classmates did the same. By following him, they gradually turned their fear of water into a love of swimming. During the last week of class, most of them were getting ready early, smiling when they came through the gate and yelling, "Watch me. I can do it!"

The only way to overcome fear is by doing something different. You can sit on the sidelines of life like a small child, sitting on the pool deck, clutching his towel to his chest, or you can "get wet." If you're going to be in the "swim of things" with a troublemaker, you have to stand up to him. You can't expect yourself to do it perfectly in the beginning, but like my little swimming students, you have to start taking steps. The first step is to be honest with yourself about how you feel when he says or does hurtful things. Your relationship will not improve if you deny your feelings and make excuses for his cruel, insensitive comments.

The second step is to tell him what he said or did, how you felt, and ask him to treat you differently from now on. Remember, we teach people how to treat us. Everything from the words we use, to our body language, our posture, our expressions and what we let them get away with teaches them how to treat us. If we want to be treated with respect, we must first treat ourselves with respect by honoring our feelings and asking for what we want.

Every time we stand up to a troublemaker, we are better prepared to do it again. Our fears disappear as we prove to ourselves that we can take care of our emotional self.

Our subconscious minds are programmed by intensity of our experiences and repetition. Every time my young swimming students mastered a new step, they felt good about themselves. That night they went to sleep, and their subconscious minds reinforced their success. The next day they returned to class where they practiced their new skill. Doing something that in the beginning looked impossible and doing it repeatedly was an intense, repetitious act that was programmed into their subconscious, where it could never be forgotten. We can use this powerful part of our mind to do the same when it comes to dealing with troublemakers. For a peacemaker, standing up to troublemakers is an intense experience. Doing it repeatedly gives the subconscious mind the repetition it needs to create a new, good habit. After we've used assertiveness skills with troublemakers for a short time, we become like my students: "Watch me. I can do it!"

The first few times you have your say with a troublemaker, you might feel guilty. The guilt feeling comes from your subconscious mind where all our feelings are housed. The reason you feel guilty is you're going against the peace-at-any-price philosophy you adopted for yourself when you were young and scared. The guilt does not mean you're doing something that is wrong. It means you're doing something that is different.

Changing the way you interact with troublemakers begins with your thought processes. Think of your mind as a garden and your thoughts as what you're planting. In a real garden we know we can't plant onions and expect roses to bloom. So, if you want to have the strength you need to stand up to anyone, you need to think of yourself as strong and worthy.

It's also important to eliminate the word "don't" from your thoughts. Telling yourself, "Don't be scared," is not helpful; our subconscious minds do not comprehend negative words. If I tell you, "Don't think about pink elephants," you immediately start to think about pink elephants. Instead of telling yourself what *not* to do, picture yourself confronting your troublemaker with your truth. In your mind's eye, see yourself looking strong and feeling courageous as you tell him what's in your heart.

When negative thoughts come into your mind, talk back to them. If your old way of thinking says, "I can't stand up to him," replace that thought with, "I can take care of my emotional self." If you 're feeling hopeless about your marriage and catch yourself thinking that it will never get any better, replace the thought with, "I can improve all my relationships by changing my responses." If you think, "I'll always be poor," replace the thought with, "I can create all the abundance my heart desires." Remember, we have attracted the troublemakers and subsequent difficult situations in our lives by the way we think and act. If we want to improve our lives, we must reprogram our subconscious minds by changing the way we think.

Our subconscious minds do not reason. They simply believe whatever we tell them. Therefore, it's extremely important for us to stop saying anything negative about ourselves. The next time you make a mistake, please do not say, "I'm so stupid," because your subconscious will believe you. These kinds of messages lower your self-esteem and impede your progress.

A few years ago I started working part-time for a company that teaches seminars for behavioral change. Our objectives are to help people stop smoking and lose weight. To do this, we give seminars that teach behavior modification and hypnosis. We explain the habitual power of the subconscious that triggers smokers to want to light up — after a meal, with an alcoholic beverage, on the phone, in the car, after sex, etc. Because their subconscious minds associate smoking with these activities, smokers automatically reach for a cigarette when they do these things.

During these seminars smokers experience a live, group hypnosis that gives them strong messages about the negative consequences of smoking as well as the positive rewards of becoming a non-smoker. Afterward, they discover that hypnosis blocks their automatic responses. Because they've been smoking for a long time and their subconscious wants to do what it's always done, we provide them with a hypnotic tape and recommend that they listen to it daily for the first 30 days. We also offer free repeats.

We are in their area every month, and any time they wish to re-attend a seminar, they can do so for free. Many of our participants return to share their success stories. A 73-year-old woman said she'd been smoking at least two and a half packs a day for over 50 years. She said she quit cold turkey after the seminar and has no desire to smoke. A 55-year-old executive said he smoked four packs a day since he was a teenager, and our seminar and tape cured his bad habit. I've heard hundreds of our seminar participants report similar results.

Our weight-loss seminars also alter lives. During the seminar, we ask our participants where they learned how to eat. Most of them say at home, where they were told to clean their plates and their parents rewarded them with dessert. We explain that this message from well-meaning parents is in their subconscious mind and puts them in conflict with their conscious mind that knows they need to lose weight. The live hypnosis and hypnotic tape we use tells them the positive rewards of attaining permanent slenderness as well as the negative consequences of being overweight.

After their subconscious absorbs these truths, their conscious and subconscious minds are in harmony and their desire for greasy, fattening, energy-draining foods goes away. Consequently, they make better food choices and lose weight. Many of them return to share their success. They report losing 30, 40, 50 pounds or more in a year, keeping it off and feeling much happier with their new life-style which includes healthy eating, moderate exercise and increased self-esteem.

Hypnosis is an excellent way to reprogram the subconscious mind. However, most of us are too busy to spend a lot of time in hypnosis. But we can change the program in our subconscious by changing our thoughts, words and actions. I quit smoking long before I studied hypnosis. Instead of being hypnotized every time I craved a cigarette, I simply told myself that I was a non-smoker and as a non-smoker I'd have more energy, vitality and self-esteem. I also told myself that I'd have fewer health problems and wrinkles, and whiter teeth. Within a few weeks my desire to smoke was almost gone. On the rare occasion, when the desire to smoke returned, I again let myself know why I was choosing to be a non-smoker — and my cravings disappeared!

If we want to get rid of our peace-at-any-price bad habit, we can start by changing the way we think. Because our subconscious mind works 24 hours a day and believes everything it hears, reading positive affirmations before going to sleep is an excellent way to reprogram our unconscious mind.

The best affirmations are the ones we write for ourselves; they address our specific problems. For instance, if your boss is one of the troublemakers in your life, you might write an affirmation that says, "I deserve to be treated with respect at work." If you too often give in to your wife because she is more aggressive than you, an affirmation that says, "I take care of myself by telling my wife how I feel and by asking for what I want," will serve you well.

Also, during our waking hours when our old, all-too-familiar negative and fearful thoughts come to mind, we need to replace them with positive, energy-giving thoughts. Thoughts of lack, limitation and hopelessness should immediately be replaced with thoughts of abundance, possibilities and expectancy. As we continue to do this, we change the way we think and act, and eventually our feelings catch up. Feelings that used to make us want to deny and avoid our fears, then encourage us to confront the people, places and things that scare us. Before we know it, we've become like the little ones I taught to swim. Inside ourselves we're saying, "Watch me. I can do it!"

REFLECTIONS

1. Based on how they treat you, make lists of who loves you and who loves you not.

2. Write about what you like about yourself and read those words before going to sleep every night.

Chapter 12

If We Make Someone Else's Problem Our Problem, Solving It Will Be Impossible

I heard Polly saying goodbye to Connie and waited for her to stick her head in my office. The lift I get from watching her overcome her dysfunctional past and grow into her potential was worth giving up the time I set aside to get paperwork done.

She looked like she'd lost a few more pounds. She was probably close to her goal weight. I asked her how Annie was doing.

"Well, she's moved out. So, I'm not sure. She's living with a binge buddy, but at least she doesn't have to listen to her father. Connie said that it's good for her to have more responsibilities and expenses, less money to spend on bingeing. I asked Connie which she thought was worse — anorexia or bulimia—"

"What did Connie say?" I asked.

"She said Annie has traded one poor coping skill for another, and both of them cause serious consequences. She said Annie experienced one of the dangers of anorexia when she broke her tailbone. Then she told me something I'd never thought about, but it makes sense. She said that by forcing herself to vomit, Annie is indirectly expressing some of the anger she feels. So, it might be a little better than being anorexic. She made me aware of how forcing oneself to vomit is a violent act, an act that helps Annie get rid of some of her rage. And she was honest with me about the dangers of bulimia. She said it causes electrolyte imbalance that can cause heart problems. She also said Annie could rupture her esophogas and bleed to death. And she said that purging puts her at high risk for developing Crohn's disease, diabetes, osteoporosis and kidney failure. These are hard things for a mother to hear, but I'd rather know the truth. And she gave me words of reassurance — which she always does."

"What did she say?"

"She said I was doing my part by treating my co-dependency. She told me to think of my family as the figures in a mobile that we put over a baby's crib and to realize that moving just one of the figures forces the others to move. By changing myself, I'm forcing Ty, Annie and Sammy to bounce around."

"Do you see that happening?" I asked.

"Oh, yeah. Because I'm no longer using food to force my feelings down, I feel better about myself, so, I don't let Ty get away with putting me down. When he says something snide or sarcastic to me, I let him know how I feel. He doesn't seem so cocky and self-assured. He seems nervous and uptight. And, of course, Annie moved out. Connie said she may have felt freer to leave, less need to stay and protect me; for the first time, she sees me taking care of myself."

"And how about your son? Has he changed?"

"Remember, I told you that he was calling me lazy, and you told me to stop defending myself. You said the truth needs no defense."

"I remember," I said.

"Well, he tried it again. He came home from school and called me lazy. I said to him, 'You're right. All I do is watch soap operas and eat bonbons.' He left the room. I couldn't see his expression. But the next day he gave me a box of bon bons. He hasn't called me lazy since then."

At that, we both laughed.

Then, I said, "The last time we talked you started to tell me about injured parts of yourself. You said you gave them Indian names. That sounds interesting. Tell me more."

"I know it sounds silly, but it works for me. I took a good, hard look at myself and my life. It made me realize that I had developed some injured parts of myself in response to what happened to me, while I was growing up in an alcoholic family. My father's drinking made him unpredictable. Sometimes he was in a good mood and generous. Other times, especially as I grew older, he was in a mean mood and was apt to do anything, even punch my mother with his fist. When he was like that, we ran away. We usually went to my grandmother's house. So, I nicknamed the part of me that's afraid of anger, the part of me that wants to run away, Running Scared. When Running Scared is in control of me, I don't stand up to Ty. All he has to do is give me a dirty look, and Running Scared wants to get away from him. Also, when she's in charge, I swallow my anger. Then, I feel resentful, and I get depressed. So, I can't afford to let Running Scared run my life."

She continued, "Shortly before I graduated from high school — around the time I met Ty — my mother died. I think the stress of putting up with Dad killed her. I call the part of me that lived through that Abandoned Adolescent. It was during this same time that I started to medicate my emotions with food. I never had a weight problem before Mom died. And I never grieved her death. Everyone said she was better off in heaven, so, I thought it would be selfish of me to cry for her. Connie is helping me to give myself permission to grieve my loss. I still miss her." Polly stopped to wipe a tear from her cheek.

I said, "It's okay to feel. Give yourself time to have your feelings."

A few more tears spilled onto her cheeks, while she fought to regain her composure. Then, she said, "When my children were born, I really missed Mom. I felt like I finally had something to give her, and she wasn't there to receive her gifts. Sometimes I try to imagine her interacting with Annie and Sam."

She shook her head, as though she was trying to chase her feelings away.

Again, I asked her to take time to feel.

She stayed with her feelings for a minute or two, then said, "When this injured part of me is in charge, I think I can't live without Ty. She makes me ignore his abuse, give in to his unreasonable demands and pretend that none of this matters. Needless to say, I can't afford to let her run the show, either. So, I've created a new part; and I call her Preferred Princess. She knows that our thoughts create our actions, and our actions create our lives. She's the more mature part of me who has decided to take care of me."

Once more she paused, this time in contemplation, it seemed.

At last, she went on, saying, "Preferred Princess knows that Ty manipulates, isolates and instigates. And she's determined to not let him get away with these things anymore. He manipulates me into spending time with him by telling me what he knows I want to hear. For instance, we'll spend a romantic evening together. He gets me to stay home then ignores me. Preferred Princess now has a Plan A and a Plan B in her head.

"When Ty says we're going to spend a romantic evening together, she goes along with the Plan which she calls, 'A.' As soon as Ty starts ignoring her, she follows with Plan B, which is to go do something nice for herself. Sometimes I go shopping. Other times I call a friend, and we go get something to eat or see a movie. Using Plan B helps me to feel less disappointed, and it gets rid of my resentments immediately."

"Wow, what a great way to see yourself as you are and to control your life!" I exclaimed.

"Preferred Princess knows the difference between wants and needs. I still want the fantasy relationship with Ty that I created in my head, but I don't need it. I can live without it. What I need is a roof over my head, food, clothes and myself. I have allowed Ty to isolate me. I gave in to him so much that I lost myself. Now I'm trying to find me."

"You're not just trying to find yourself," I said, "you're rediscovering yourself—"

"Well, I am doing better. I followed Connie's suggestion to write my feelings in my journal every day." She flipped to the back of her journal and showed me a list of affirmations. "I made these up myself," she said. "I read them every night before I go to sleep."

"Read some of them to me," I said.

Polly began with, "My feelings are my friends. Like my senses, they protect me. I honor them. I keep my focus on my thoughts, feelings and actions because I am the only person I can control. I live one day at a time. I eat small portions of fruits, vegetables, whole grains and lean meats at regular intervals to satisfy my hunger. I drink eight glasses of water daily. I make time to exercise, sleep and have fun. I rely on a spiritual power for strength and guidance. No one can make me feel bad about myself without my permission. The last one I stole from Eleanor Roosevelt. I then say the Serenity Prayer."

"I'm sure Connie told you why it helps to say these affirmations before falling asleep —"

"Oh, yes. She said bedtime is the best time, since my subconscious mind never sleeps, and it will believe whatever I tell it. I've noticed a difference in myself since I started saying them less than a month ago. In fact, I'm taking a couple of courses at our community college. I thought I'd feel strange going back to school, you know, thinking I was too old. But there are quite a few people there my age. I don't feel odd. I feel like I'm doing something good for myself."

"And you are! You're facing your fears, taking control of your life and realizing that you can make good decisions for yourself. Best of all, you're minding your own business, not wasting your life trying to fix Ty or Annie."

"I do feel better."

"Great!"

She gave me a big hug and went on her way.

No Decision Is a Decision

After Polly left, I thought about an Al-Ateen group that I sponsored more than 10 years ago. We met every Sunday evening. Each week, one of the group — teenagers of at least one alcoholic parent — was in charge of picking the topic they wanted to discuss. In the more than five years that we met, the only topics they ever chose to discuss were anger and procrastination.

Growing up in an alcoholic family helped me understand their need to talk about feeling angry towards a parent who drank too much, embarrassed them, constantly changed the rules and punished them harshly for things they did and didn't do. Understanding their desire to discuss procrastination took longer. But as I got more in touch with myself, as I understood my wish to please everyone, I appreciated why they procrastinated.

Some of these teens were peace-at-any-price people like me. More than anything, they wanted the fighting and arguing in their homes to stop. They were willing to do whatever it took to "keep the peace." In their quest to please everyone, they felt confused. Decision-making was extremely difficult since they did not want to displease anyone. Thus, if they thought one person wanted them to do something and another person wanted them to do something different, they couldn't please them both. Therefore, they tried not to make any decision, thus protecting themselves from the consequences of disappointing anyone. Many of them tried to solve this problem by spending lots of time alone. In isolation, they were more at peace; they weren't trying to do the impossible — please all the people all of the time.

Many of the brothers and sisters of these peace-at-any-price kids were their opposites. They were more in touch with the anger they felt, and they didn't want to please anyone. Making waves helped them express their anger. However, when it comes to making decisions, not wanting to please anyone can pose as much of a problem as wanting to please everyone. It's as difficult to make decisions that will displease everyone as it is to make decisions that please everyone. Because every action begins with a decision, they too procrastinated.

The good news is — by getting together — the teens in the Al-Ateen group broke the don't talk rule. By talking openly and honestly about their home lives, they were able to at least identify that procrastinating was responsible for their failing grades. Some of them stopped blaming their parents, took more responsibility for themselves and earned some of the freedoms they yearned for by improving their grades and doing their chores.

While I was the Al-Ateen group facilitator, I came across a story about procrastination and shared it with them. In the story, which takes place a long time ago, a widowed mother shares a small cabin with her teenage son. The young fellow is always tired. His mother is worried about his health since he never seems to have any energy. He is always resting. So, she takes him to their doctor for an examination.

After examining the boy, the doctor confronts the mother and says, "This lad is exhausted. What do you make him do?"

The mother is offended by the doctor's words, and she replies, "I do all the work. He has just one chore. He brings the wood in and makes a fire in our wood-burning stove so that I can cook our evening meal."

The doctor frowns, scratches his head, then asks, "When does he do this chore?"

The mother answers, "He always waits until the last minute."

The doctor smiles and says, "That's the problem. He's carrying the wood all day"

REFLECTIONS

1. Can you identify injured parts of yourself and give them names?

2. Identify the consequences you've suffered when you've allowed these injured parts to run your life.

3. Are you a procrastinator? If so, identify why it's difficult for you to make decisions.

Chapter 13

Life Is Best Lived
One Moment at a Time

Thinking about standing up to troublemakers scares peacemakers. Knowing how often troublemakers get angry to get their way makes us want to continue to avoid arguments, dodge debates and do all we can to keep the peace. We justify our desire to do these things by saying, "It's not worth it." We can translate, "It's not worth it," into, "I'm not worth it," if we allow anyone to rob us of the serenity, dignity and joy we can have by claiming it. Remember, we can change any relationship by changing the way we interact. We are part of the problem if we allow anyone to be disrespectful to us.

The best way to change your reactions to troublemakers is one incident and one moment at a time. If the thought of standing your ground with troublemakers seems like an insurmountable task, you haven't broken it down into small, manageable steps. Everything we learn to do, we do one step at a time. Perhaps reading this book is your *first* step.

The next step is to be brutally honest with yourself about how you feel when someone — anyone — is disrespectful to you. We, who obeyed society's dysfunctional rules by keeping our mouths shut for a long, long time, often do not even know what we're feeling. We are accustomed to putting the wants and needs of others so far ahead of our own that we may not know what we desire. This needs to change. We need to slow down, give up the food, drink, always keeping busy, whatever our emotional medication of choice is, and get in touch with ourselves. Remember, if nothing changes, then nothing changes.

By being silent, by allowing troublemakers to get their way, we are part of the problem. Only when we stand up for ourselves, when we are strong enough to take care of our emotional selves, as Polly is doing, can we make a difference. If we allow anyone to take advantage of us, to rob us of the peace we yearn for, to treat us poorly, we are not giving that person any incentive to change. Consequently, we will continue to live in a tumultuous world governed by troublemakers.

The peace on Earth begins inside each one of us. And those of us who were traumatized at an early age and, therefore, adopted a peace-at-any-price philosophy, need to examine the pitfalls of such a philosophy. We need to realize that our best efforts to keep the peace have failed and embark on a new way of creating the peace we want most.

Step three is to use assertiveness skills. Every time someone calls you names, yells at you, uses sarcasm or is insensitive to your feelings, you need to tell that person what he said or did that offended you. Your reason for doing this is to take care of your emotional self, not to change the other person. You cannot expect to feel and perform at your best if you allow anyone to hurt you emotionally.

Next, you need to identify and tell that person your feelings. Please, do not say, "You made me feel . . ." because no one can make us feel anything, though we all feel. Simply say, "I felt . . ." Own your feelings. They're a wonderful part of you. They'll help you to care for yourself if you honor them.

The last step is to ask for what you want. You might say, "I want you to speak to me in a normal tone of voice." Making this request does not guarantee that the other person will change the way he treats you. It does guarantee, though, that you will become emotionally stronger, more internally focused and better prepared to take care of yourself in any situation.

Peace-at-any-price people are not quick on their feet. Early on in our lives we learned to shut down when someone big and scary got mad. Consequently, as adults, our knee-jerk reaction is to get very quiet when others are upset.

Fortunately, there are no statue of limitations on using assertiveness skills. Whenever you get in touch with how you felt, you need to take care of yourself by mentioning the incident to the troublemaker, state how you felt and ask for what you want from now on.

Don't justify your desire to remain silent under such circumstances by telling yourself some stupid cliché like "Let sleeping dogs lie" or "Don't make waves." And don't tell yourself that the incident is over and done. It doesn't matter how long ago it occurred. What matters is that you care for yourself emotionally by telling the troublemaker exactly what happened, how you felt and ask for what you want. Remember, feelings do not magically disappear. They have the power to make us healthy or sick, strong or weak, happy or sad, productive or stagnant. If we want to feel good, we must honor them by being truthful.

Every time you take care of your emotional self by using assertiveness skills, your subconscious mind makes a record of your brave words. The next time you are in a situation that requires you to stand up for yourself, your subconscious lets you know that you've done this before. Thus, using assertiveness skills gets easier and easier, just like anything else you've mastered.

Potential Has a Shelf Life

Peace-at-any-price people are guilty of wishing and hoping that the troublemakers in their life will change. These same reasonable people, who take responsibility for paying their bills, cleansing their bodies, eating good nutrition and keeping their minds and bodies active, allow others to damage them emotionally by failing to use assertiveness skills. They accept what they learned about keeping the peace, obey society's dysfunctional rules and rely on substances and activities to medicate the emotions that are forever urging them to have their say and be who they are. Just wishing and hoping doesn't change anything. And the feelings we stuff are like lava in a volcano that erupts at unexpected times and hurts innocent people.

I am a recovering peace-at-any-price person who feels much better since I have given up hoping that anyone else will change. Instead of wasting precious moments and energy wishing for anyone but me to change, I use my time and energy to better myself and my life. I know that other people will change when the pain caused by what they are doing becomes greater than their fear of change. To help them with this process, I try never to give them a pay off for their negative words and actions.

The most common complaint I receive from clients who I encourage to recognize that others will grow into their potential when they're ready and not until is, "That's hard to do." I agree with them. Hard, yes, but not impossible. Trying to change another person is impossible. Would you rather attempt what's difficult or what's impossible? Do you prefer to lose your happiness waiting for someone to change or create happiness by becoming all you can be? And what's worthwhile that you have accomplished in life that was easy?

What makes changing ourselves and our reactions difficult are two thieves that I call *If Only* and *What If*.

If Only is the part of us that reminds us of our mistakes. He's a Monday-morning quarterback who lives in yesterday and tells us our life would be different if we had done such and such. He makes us think that there's nothing we can do to alter today because of the choices we made in the past. He doesn't acknowledge that life is a growth and change process, and we all make mistakes. Our so-called mistakes were experiences that afforded us opportunities to learn lessons. If we made poor choices, we suffered consequences. Therefore, we need not punish ourselves with guilt, shame and regrets.

When we listen to If Only, we feel hopeless and destined to continue doing what we've always done — even accept abuse from a "loved one." Have you ever caught yourself saying, "That's the way I am," as if you do not have the power to change yourself? The person you were yesterday is not the person you are today, unless you stubbornly hold on to him or her and insist that you cannot change yourself.

Some of If Only's favorite lines are:

If Only I'd been born rich.

If Only I'd gone to college.

If Only I'd married someone else.

If Only I'd bought a house.

If Only I never started smoking.

This negative, excuse-making part of us that clings to yesterday is out of touch with reality. In reality, we can change yesterday by changing the way we view it, and every new moment gives us an opportunity to make better choices.

We can stay stuck in the past and feel hopeless by listening to If Only. Or we can talk back to him. We can replace what he says with hopeful messages such as, "It's never too late to change what I dislike" or "I can create more wealth, better relationships, a nicer place to live, a better job, anything I want."

Sometimes If Only reminds us of something we did that hurt someone. If that person is still living, you can silence If Only by apologizing to him or her and vowing never to treat anyone that way again. Even the Almighty forgives us for mistakes we acknowledge and vow not to repeat because that is all we can do. Allowing these mistakes to cripple us with guilt does not make anything better. If the one you hurt is deceased, offer your sincere apology in a prayer and let it go. The best restitution you can make is to live in today in a new and better way.

I have clients who embrace If Only. They insist upon giving their power to him in spite of what I say. I refuse to listen to them plead their case too many times since their subconscious mind believes what it hears them say. Instead of letting them use me as a sounding board to put a negative, hopeless message in their minds, I explain how our subconscious works and suggest several ways for them to make positive changes in themselves. If they refuse to accept any of my suggestions, I tell them I can't help them and send them on their way.

The second thief I call *What If*

What If is If Only's noisy younger brother who lives in tomorrow. He's so busy worrying about what might happen tomorrow that he doesn't enjoy or take responsibility for today.

What If is a wet blanket. He likes to douse the spark of every idea. He is to ideas what the Grinch is to Christmas. He extinguishes the excitement of every new thought by telling us what might go wrong.

Logically, I know that what What If says is not true because every time I take a risk, I emerge stronger, more knowledgeable and better prepared to take on new challenges. I know that it is only by doing something new that I can improve my life and the lives of others. But What If is not logical. He is fearful. His goal is to reduce my life to a monotonous, humdrum existence. He will drown my dreams if I give my power to him.

I talk back to What If by recalling some of the favorable outcomes of risks I took in the past. One of my favorites took place on a cold January day in the early 1960s when I was living with a roommate in New York City, We both worked for Eastern Air Lines. We each had one dollar in our purse, the next day off, bare cupboards and a desire to live life to the fullest. Not knowing how we could afford to even eat the next day with so little money, no checkbooks, credit cards or uncollected debts, we decided to use an airline pass and go to San Juan, Puerto Rico.

We each spent 15 cents for the subway and another 15 cents for the bus that took us to Kennedy Airport. We boarded the first-class section of a non-stop, champagne-breakfast flight that served fruit, eggs benedict, muffins and coffee. At the San Juan Airport, we spent a quarter for a locker to store our travel clothes and used the rest room to change into swimsuits, t-shirts, shorts and sneakers. Then, we walked about three miles to a beach behind the Holiday Inn where we ran into a couple of Eastern ticket agents enjoying their day off water skiing. They shared their boat and skis with us and gave us a ride back to the airport in time to board the six o'clock, non-stop, first-class flight home. The stewardesses served us free cocktails and a delicious surf-and-turf dinner. After landing at Kennedy, we spent another 30 cents each for the bus and connecting subway transportation to get back to our apartment. We arrived home around ten o'clock wearing a suntan and a smile.

If we had allowed What If to be in charge of our thinking, we would not have gone to San Juan for the day.

Now that I'm older and wiser, I think about going all the way to Puerto Rico with nothing but a dollar in my pocket, and I let What If speak.

She says, "What If you got mugged?"

I say, "It's better to be mugged if you have nothing for the thief to take."

What If says, "What if the plane went down?"

I answer, "What can money do to make a plane crash better?"

Think about your challenges. Think about anything you want to accomplish. Do you want to lose weight? If so, don't think, I'm going to lose 20, 30, 40 pounds, because the thought of such an enormous task will overwhelm you and make you want to quit. Instead say, "Just for today I will eat nutritious, energy-giving foods, drink lots of water and get some exercise."

Do you want to stand up to a troublemaker. If you answer, "Yes," don't say,

"From now on I'm going to tell him or her what's on my mind." Instead say, "I will care for myself emotionally, one minute and one incident at a time."

REFLECTIONS

1. Write what your *If Only* says to you.

2. Write what your *What If* says to you.

3. Replace these fearful, negative messages with positive, energy-giving thoughts and say them to yourself every night before falling asleep.

4. Recall times in your life when you silenced these two thieves, lived for the moment and thoroughly enjoyed life.

Chapter 14

By Being Compassionate with Myself, I Develop Compassion for Others

The cause of much cruelty in our society is our adherence to the "don't-talk" and "don't-feel" rules. Because we are not encouraged to express our emotions in healthy, straightforward ways, some people use road rage and other acts of aggression and violence to rid themselves of pent-up feelings. Others learned that keeping the peace is the same as keeping their mouths shut. Their best attempts to deny and avoid anger leaves them feeling anxious. Occasionally, their anger spews forth like lava from a volcano and injures innocent people. Still others use sarcasm, snide remarks and passive-aggressive behaviors to indirectly dispatch their wrath. The feelings we stuff will not magically disappear; we are forced to use healthy or unhealthy ways to deal with them.

Unfortunately, far too many of us think we are being selfish if we have our say and ask for what we want. If you're a person who thinks you must always put the wants and needs of others ahead of your own, keep in mind that you cannot give to others what you don't have. If your pockets are empty, you don't have a dollar to give to charity. If you're wearing your old clothes, you have none to give to the Salvation Army. If you are not sensitive to your feelings and compassionate with yourself, you have no sensitivity or compassion to give to others.

If you swallow your emotions, pretend they don't exist, you will automatically ask others to do the same. No man or woman is sensitive to others until he or she becomes sensitive to himself/herself.

The fact that we are doing what we've been taught, what we've always done, does not make our words and actions any less harmful and hurtful. Knowing that our feelings, habits and much of our ability is under wraps in our unconscious mind does not mean that we are not responsible for how we think and act. We all have the ability to gradually bring forth what's stored in our subconscious minds, review it, keep what we want and toss the rest out.

To better understand how powerful our subconscious minds are, if you know how to type, draw a keyboard and try to consciously write down the location of each key. Notice how difficult that task is. Yet, you can put your fingers on the keyboard and type without even looking at the keys. As an experiment, move your waste can and notice how many times in the next month your unconscious takes you to where the can used to be.

If we want to create peace on Earth, we cannot allow our powerful, habitual, subconscious minds, which have been programmed with self-defeating information, to run our lives. We cannot depend upon the old, erroneous information stored in this part of our brain to dictate our thoughts and actions. Instead we must reprogram our minds the same way we reprogram our computers. We must bring up on a screen (our mind's eye) the information that no longer serves us well and press delete. Then, we need to continuously put in the positive data that will help us turn our lives into the peaceful, exciting adventures they were meant to be.

If We Always Do What We've Always Done, Nothing Changes

Changing anything, even ourselves, is not easy. Yet, everything and everyone is designed to change. Telling yourself not to grow and change is like telling the leaves on trees not to turn into color, fall to the ground and make room for new buds.

If you are a peace-at-any-price person, you may be allowing your inner robot

— alias your subconscious mind — to have too much to say. Perhaps you grew up in a violent family or one that down-played the importance of expressing emotions. Consequently, you decided that you will keep your complaints to yourself and get others to do your will by always being nice, always doing what they want, even compromising some of your morals, values and principles to keep the peace with them. Have you noticed that your best efforts have not worked?

Perhaps you've tucked your chin in and begun to console yourself with the cliché, "Nice guys finish last." Keeping your thoughts to yourself, giving in to troublemakers, allowing anyone to take advantage of you or to treat you with disrespect does not mean you're a nice guy or gal. It means you need to get more in touch with yourself, be who you are and stop allowing anyone to diminish you.

Sometimes the motivation behind a peace-at-any-price person's words and actions is a desire to get other people's approval. One of life's best ironies is we do not win anyone's approval — until we stop asking for it. No one promotes placaters, celebrates cowards or worships wimps. It's the people who know who they are and what they want that we look up to. They're the ones who get what they want out of life.

If we want to create the peace on Earth that begins inside each one of us, we need to first examine our motives. We need to ask ourselves why we say, "Yes," when we feel, "No." We need to look objectively at our lives. If they're not all we want them to be, we need to take responsibility for changing the way we think and act. We must refuse to give our power away by blaming God, the devil, fate or troublemakers and realize that we are the masters of our destiny. If we have troublemakers in our lives, we have attracted them to us. If we want them to treat us with respect, we must protect our dignity by using assertiveness skills and setting boundaries.

In the beginning, when you start standing up for yourself — if you feel scared — remind yourself of the alternatives. If you fail to take care of your emotional self, the anger you swallow will turn into depression. The fear you fail to acknowledge and overcome will turn into anxiety. Both depression and anxiety, which we commonly refer to as stress, can make us sick.

Growing up in an alcoholic, violent family provided me with an opportunity to witness the power of emotions early. My mother and one of my brothers seemed fine when Dad was out of town. As soon as they heard his truck coming down our street, neither one of them could catch their breath. They both reached for their inhalers to stave off an asthma attack. My mother left this world early, at age 43, while gasping for air. My brother's asthma disappeared after he left home. Acknowledging the connection between crippling emotions and poor health helped me to reach out for help when I had colitis, difficulty breathing and ached all over.

The help I received from counselors, support groups and friends made me realize that we had been a family living in quicksand. We couldn't lift each other up. Finally, when I reached up, first to God and then to the "soldiers" He surrounded me with, those who were standing on the bank, I had an opportunity to break the "don't-talk" and "don't-feel" rules and to develop a philosophy that serves me better than my peace-at-any-price philosophy. Since then, I've worked at staying out of the quicksand, and I am sometimes awarded the pleasure of extending my hand to someone who wants to be lifted up.

I must admit, in the beginning, putting my well being first, doing what was best for me, honoring my feelings and having my say felt selfish. I often struggled with guilt and prayed for strength and guidance. Gradually, my peace-at-any-price ways of thinking and acting went away. I know they will not return, since I cannot have compassion for anyone else unless I am compassionate with myself. If I try to cover up my feelings, pretend they don't exist, I automatically want others to do the same. I cannot be comfortable with their expression of feelings unless I am comfortable with my own.

Change is always uncomfortable. Our subconscious minds, the robots within, the part of us that knows which song is coming next when we're listening to a favorite CD compels us to want to do what we've always done. This is especially true when it comes to something as difficult for an adult raised in our society as expressing our feelings honestly. But if we refuse to challenge ourselves, if we allow our unconscious minds to win, we put ourselves in conflict with our God-given soul that knows we need to be treated with respect to preserve our dignity. Allowing anyone to emotionally abuse us lowers our self-esteem and puts us at risk for developing addictions, eating disorders, anxiety, depression and physical illnesses.

Polly is just one of many clients I've worked with who dramatically changed her life and all her relationships by changing herself. The last time I saw her she said, "Annie and I are going to Weight Watchers together, and it was Annie's idea. Ty and Sammy are still trying to get my goat, but it isn't working." She said she'd stopped telling them where her goat was. We laughed.

Polly had lost her tense need for control and found her sense of humor.

Payoffs for Overcoming a Peace-At-Any-Price Personality

1. You'll stop attracting troublemakers. You probably have enough of them in your life. You don't need any more.

2. Changing the way you react to a troublemaker may give them incentive to change themselves. People change when the pain they endure as a result of what they're doing exceeds their fear of change. Troublemakers have no desire to change if they can bully you into doing their will.

3. By giving up all attempts to do the impossible (change anyone else), you free up the time and energy you need to improve yourself and your life.

4. You'll have fewer disappointments if you expect less from others. Remember, an expectation is a resentment waiting to happen.

5. Making decisions is easy when you stop trying to do the impossible, and that is: Please all the people all the time.

6. The choices we make shape our lives. Making the right choices for yourself guarantees that you'll live a life that's right for you.

REFLECTIONS

1. List 10 things you can do to be more compassionate with yourself.

Recommended Reading

The references below are for the original hardcover edition of each title listed (where available). Be aware that your local library or bookstore may be able to get these titles for you by different publishers in a variety of bindings, sizes and types, including large print, audio cassette, CD, softcover, mass market and more.

Drews, Toby Rice. *Getting Them Sober: A Guide for Those Who Live with an Alcoholic*, Vol. 1. Haven Books, 1980.

Dyer, Wayne. *Pulling Your Own Strings: Dynamic Techniques for Dealing with Other People and Living Your Life as You Choose*. HarperTorch, 1994.

Fitzgerald, Kathleen Whalen. *Alcoholism, The Genetic Inheritance*. Wales' Tale Press, 1988.

Gibran, Kahil, *The Prophet*. Knopf, 1923.

Gray, John. *Children Are From Heaven: Positive Parenting Skills for Raising Cooperative, Confident, and Compassionate Children*. HarperCollins, 1999.

Hendrix, Harville. *Getting The Love You Want: A Guide for Couples*. Smithmark Pub., 1988.

Kirshenbaum, Mira. *Too Good To Leave, Too Bad To Stay: A Step-by-Step Guide to Helping You Decide Whether to Stay In or Get Out of Your Relationship*. Dutton Books, 1996.

Mason, Paul T., and Randi Kreger. *Stop Walking On Eggshells: Coping When Someone You Care About Has Borderline Personality Disorder*. New Harbinger Publications, Inc., 1998.

Milam, James R., and Katherine Ketcham. *Under The Influence: A Guide to the Myths and Realities of Alcoholism*. Slawson Communications, 1981.

Murphy, Joseph. *The Power of Your Subconscious Mind*. 2001. Simon & Schuster, 1963.

Roth, Geneen. *When Food Is Love: Exploring the Relationship Between Eating and Intimacy*. Penguin, 1991.

Walsh, Neale Donald. *Conversations With God: An Uncommon Dialogue* (vols. 1, 2 & 3). 1996. Putnam Publishing Group, 1996.

Websites:

www.AdultChildrenOfAlcoholics.com

www.AlcoholicsAnonymous.com

www.Al-Anon.com

www.Anorexia.com

www.Bulimia.com

www.NationalEatingDisorders.com

www.WellnessSeminars.org

Index

About the Author

Deborah Day Poor, LCSW, says she was held hostage during her childhood by her abusive, alcoholic father. At 18 she left home thinking she'd left her past behind. In time, she realized that she was recreating relationships similar to the one she left.

Deborah Day Poor, LCSW

With therapeutic individual and group help, Deborah found the strength she needed to overcome her peace-at-any-price personality and begin college at age 41. She graduated *magnum cum laude* from the University of South Florida and obtained a Masters Degree in Clinical Social Work from Florida State University. She is a member of the National Association of Social Workers and the Tampa Bay Association of Women Psychotherapists.

Deborah Day Poor currently works as a licensed psychotherapist in Lakeland, Florida. She has worked in addiction and eating disorder treatment centers as a primary therapist and as a clinical director. She has specialized in teaching parenting skills and treating addictions, eating disorders, and relationship dependency. She also worked as a seminar presenter, using hypnosis to help participants quit smoking and lose weight. She shares her experience, strength and hope to help her clients, students and readers become all that they can be.

Products and Services

Products

- Is someone you love really an alcoholic? ***Understanding and Treating Alcoholism*** by Deborah Day Poor (a 45-minute CD) answers this question, explains why alcoholism is a legitimate disease — not a bad habit — and tells you how to help both the alcoholic and yourself.

- Alcoholics have an 80% better chance of recovery IF their partner overcomes co-dependency. ***Facts and Fallacies of Co-dependency*** by Deborah Day Poor (a 45-minute CD) explains the difference between enabling and just being nice and tells you what you can do to improve your life and the lives of others.

CDs are $10 each or two for $18 (both options post paid). To order, visit www.bookch.com or call toll free 1-800-431-1579. For bulk purchases, contact—

Deborah Day Poor, LCSW
Post Office Box 164
Parrish, FL 34219-0164
dpoor1@tampabay.rr.com.

Services

To schedule Deborah Day Poor for civic, support and church group workshops/presentations on "How to Overcome the Please Disease" or for group/individual therapy sessions, please contact her directly by email at dpoor1@tampabay.rr.com.